MEMOIRS OF A COMEBACK TRUMPET PLAYER

a practical and evolving approach to the trumpet and jazz

Stanley D. Glick

© Copyright 2017 by Stanley D. Glick

This book may not be reproduced in any form without the written consent of the author.

Table of Contents

4	Introduction
8	Part I: Equipment
8	Mouthpieces
13	Bach
13	Parduba
14	Callet
15	Yamaha, Curry, Schilke
15	Asymmetrical
16	GR Technologies
16	Marcinkiewicz
17	Instruments
18	Trumpets: vintage vs. new, student vs. professional, light vs. heavy, medium-large bore vs. large bore
19	Trumpets: Bachs, Yamahas and Other Wild Things
26	Cornets
28	Flugelhorns
28	Footnote: the pocket trumpet
29	Mutes
29	Straight and cup mutes
30	Wah-wah mutes: "Harmon" and bubble
32	Plungers and plunger mutes
32	Practice mutes
33	Bucket mutes
33	Solotone, purdie, and derby
33	Bags, foam and other muting devices
34	Valve oils and slide greases
39	Miscellaneous accessories and treatment
39	Heavy valve caps

39	Heavy mouthpieces
40	Brass valve guides and fast spring
40	Digital valve alignment
41	Cryogenic treatment
41	Cleaning (mouthpiece and leadpipe)
43	Part II: Technical Aspects of Playing
44	Embouchure
50	Warm-ups
52	Practicing
59	Part III: Jazz Theory and Jazz
62	Learning scales and chords
65	The cycle of fifths (or fourths)
66	Contour, rhythm and essential tones
67	Jazz rhythm
68	Chromaticism
68	"Special effects
69	Playing the changes: vertical vs. horizontal
70	Inside vs. outside
70	Pentatonic shortcuts
71	The minor II-V-I
72	Tension and release
74	THE END (really the end of the beginning, or maybe the end of the middle)
75	About the Author

INTRODUCTION

Nineteen years ago, all was quiet at night. After dinner and after watching the news, my wife and I would each check our email and then do some reading before convening again for a nightcap before adjourning to bed; occasionally, instead of reading, we might watch a movie on HBO. With all our kids now out of the house, the youngest just off to college, life was becoming serene indeed. Little did I know it but an email message would soon change everything.

A new faculty member at my medical college, who happened to play the alto sax, was trying to start a "big band." The music of Ellington, Miller, and Basie beckoned him to recreate a group similar to one he had started at his previous institution. I read the email, considered my newfound freedom, and decided that it might be fun to get back into music.

I started playing trumpet when I was six years old. By the time I was eight, I was playing solos, accompanied by my piano-playing mother, at the school's spring concert. By 12 I was playing in a symphony orchestra. When I was 16, I was in a trumpet trio, playing in talent shows and occasionally winning. Along the way I was in a couple of Dixieland combos, but by 18 it was all over. I entered college, briefly played with the school orchestra, but then gave it up entirely. Other activities seemed to be more important—several years of education, raising a family, and pursuit of a career in science.

But it was more than just competing interests: I never thought I could ever really be good.

I took private trumpet lessons for 10 years, from ages 6-16. It was all primarily technical. The Arban book was the bible and my task was to master it. Although I knew I liked jazz, neither of my two trumpet teachers paid much attention to what I liked. Consequently, my daily practice session was a required ordeal, not a time for fun. And that, in retrospect, was what was missing. No one taught me or encouraged me to enjoy music. In contrast, my older brother, who actually started learning the guitar a couple of years after I started the trumpet, had a wonderful teacher; and my brother quickly became a competent jazz guitarist, playing many weekend gigs with his own combo while still in high school.

Sometimes, at family gatherings, when I was in high school and my brother was in college, we would try to play together. Most of the tunes would sound pretty decent until it was my turn to improvise. Then it was usually, though not always, a "train wreck." My ear was my guide; actually, my ear was the beginning and the end. As far as I knew at the time, improvisation was all about playing by ear, and obviously my ear was not up to par. Until nineteen years ago, I thought chords were irrelevant to being able to play the trumpet. It was no wonder that I became discouraged in my youth and gave up trying.

Turn the clock ahead 35 years. I emailed my colleague and told him that if he was willing to put up with me, and the time it would take me to relearn basic skills, I was willing to give the big band a try. Fortunately for me, he was a patient man.

I have rediscovered the trumpet, and rediscovered music (jazz in particular), during the past nineteen years. In addition to fully exploring all the many resources on the internet, I have read just about every book I could find about playing the trumpet and about playing jazz. The evenings, and/or the mornings, are no longer quiet. My daily practice routine usually lasts about two hours, or at least never less than an hour. I virtually never go anywhere for more than a day without taking a trumpet with me, usually a pocket trumpet or a cornet. The big band, called the Swing Docs, became quite successful in the Albany, NY area, where I resided until I retired a couple of years ago. The Swing Docs usually had at least one gig each month. In addition, for 15 years, I led a jazz sextet (called FIVE+1) that also was getting regular gigs. I was having fun, and enjoying music more than ever; and I'm still enjoying music, now playing with a new big band and with a trio (guitar, bass and flugelhorn) in the Tampa, FL area where I now live. And I'm playing far better than I ever thought was possible. By the way, my wife is now also having fun at making music: she became a comeback accordionist and recently started taking drum lessons!

So, what is this book about and why am I writing it? As I've said, I've read many books about the trumpet and about jazz. And I have tried to do many of the things that the books recommend. However, it is simply impossible to do everything that even one book suggests is necessary. For example, almost every book on jazz improvisation stresses the importance of learning scales, patterns and exercises in all 12 keys. If one attempted to do this as instructed, there would be little time left in the day to brush one's teeth, not to mention going to work in the non-musical world for 8-10 hours a day. It recently occurred to me that all of the books I've read in this regard are aimed at helping people become professional musicians. The authors of these books, who are all professionals, all strive for perfection; anything less is a mistake waiting to be corrected. In theory I agree with this credo. In reality there is simply not enough time. My goal, and hopefully the goal of you the reader, is to play well and have fun. The two are closely related: the better I play, the more fun I have. But time is a limiting factor, and at least until my retirement, I was unable to devote the long hours of practice required of a professional musician. This book is therefore an attempt to reach an attainable goal, to make playing well and having fun a realistic goal. In the pages that follow, I review the various approaches and techniques, as well as myths and dogma, that other authors have advanced, and I try to distill the essential truths that are most important for playing the trumpet and for playing jazz. If you're a would-be full-time professional, this is not the book for you. But if you have some basic trumpet technique and basic knowledge of jazz, this book should help you use both to better advantage.

The book is organized into three parts. The first part deals with equipment; and by "equipment" I mean anything from a $3 bottle of valve oil to a $10,000+ Monette instrument. There is no disputing the fact that equipment affects how we play; and I will try to sort out which equipment is best for which purpose. The second part deals with the technical aspects of playing, from embouchure development to playing double high C's. In between we will deal with warm-up exercises, scales and articulation studies. The third and last part deals with learning to play jazz. We will focus on distinguishing what is essential from what may be useful on occasion.

PART I: EQUIPMENT

Trumpet players love equipment and love to talk about it. Just look at any of the trumpet player bulletin boards on the internet. You can find virtually any opinion that you would want to hear about anything. Are my opinions better than any others? Possibly not, but I'm going to venture them anyway. They have all been formed on the basis of both considerable personal experience and many comments from many other trumpet players. Perhaps more important than my opinions are the reasons for my opinions. I will try to elaborate whenever possible so the reader can decide for himself/herself whether there is a rational basis for an opinion.

Mouthpieces

The perfect mouthpiece is the "holy grail" of the trumpet player. I doubt that anyone playing the trumpet for a year or more would think differently. Changing the mouthpiece can affect tone, articulation and range, and probably to a greater extent than any change in instrument. It is no wonder then that trumpet players are often obsessed with finding a better mouthpiece. "A better mouthpiece" is most often defined as one that will enable the player to reach a higher note. More on this later.

As we will discuss later, there are many different makes of trumpets, many more than there were even 40-50 years ago. This has led some observers to label this time as the "golden age of the trumpet" or, perhaps more accurately, the "golden age of trumpet making." However, borrowing from the credit card industry, this must also be the platinum age of mouthpieces or of mouthpiece making. While almost every brand of trumpet is accompanied by a same-named brand of mouthpiece, there are several small companies that primarily make mouthpieces rather than instruments. Mouthpieces differ in every conceivable way, even in the materials used; while the vast majority are brass, there are also mouthpieces made of other materials, for example, nylon (DEG), polycarbonate (Mad Max) and wood (The Perfect Wood). The most important differences between mouthpieces relate to the size and shape of the rim and the size and shape of the cup, although the size of the throat (the hole) and the shape of the backbore (the long part) are also important. So, if this is all there is to consider, wouldn't you expect that eventually every manufacturer would figure out all possible combinations and make essentially the same line of mouthpieces? Far from it—probably no two mouthpieces from any two companies are exactly the same. Why this is true is more mysterious than anyone is likely to know. Of course, every brand has its own unique explanation of why its product is the best, including the high quality of materials used, the degree of precision employed in manufacture, the use of computer modeling as well as the use of design elements that are at least unusual if not unique (for example, detachable cups and backbores, double cups, adjustable cups, heavy cups, long or short backbores etc.). Like many or most of my trumpet playing colleagues, I've been victim of the mouthpiece quest myself. Although I haven't found the perfect piece (if there is such a thing, it would probably be one that played by itself), I've searched enough to know that I've reached the end of my search.

Sixty years ago, Bach reigned supreme with regard to mouthpieces. Every horn player I knew and played with as I was growing up used a Bach mouthpiece regardless of what brand of trumpet they were using. In some respects, Bach is still the standard against which all others are compared. However, the main comparison made to the Bach relates to the size of the mouthpiece rather than its quality or playing characteristics. That is, the Bach 3C, 5C, 7C and 10½E were at one time so popular that other brands of mouthpieces routinely compare their rim and cup sizes to the Bach models. Curiously, as was the case 60 years ago, the Bach 7C is still routinely recommended as the starting mouthpiece for new trumpet players. This one-size-fits-all has never made sense and has probably been continued because no one has ever figured out an objective way of determining which size is best for which individual. Once someone has experience at playing, he or she is capable deciding for themselves which mouthpiece feels and plays best. But the choice for the novice is dependent on the mercy of tradition. Personally, I think the time has come to end this tradition. The lips of a 6-year old are likely to be much smaller than the lips of a 16-year old. It would make sense to start the younger child with a smaller mouthpiece (for example, a Bach 10) than that used for the older child; and initially, in terms of getting a sound out of the instrument, both young and old might benefit from a deeper cup (for example, a Bach B). Within a couple of months of starting, however, when the goal has changed and the student may be trying to reach higher notes, the attentive teacher should be ready to advise his or her student to try other sizes (and probably shallower cups).

Bach mouthpieces are still probably the starting point for most trumpet players beginning their personal hunt for the best piece. Once the desire arises to try other makes, the choices soon become overwhelming. The obvious differences among mouthpieces are related to their dimensions: the inner and outer diameters of the rim (which also determine the thickness of the rim), the depth of the cup (deep vs. shallow), and the size of the throat (smaller or larger hole to the backbore). Less obvious differences are related to the contour of the rim (flat or rounded), the shape of the cup (bowl shaped or V shaped, or a combination of the two), and the size and taper of the backbore. Two mouthpieces may have identical dimensions but play very differently because one has a flat rim and the other has a rounded rim. So how does one decide which is the better mouthpiece, not to mention the elusive goal of determining which is the best mouthpiece?

The solution, or the process, I recommend is a systematic version of trial-and-error; perhaps it should be called "trial-and-trial." I will elaborate.

First and foremost, the mouthpiece has to be comfortable. If you're in pain when you're playing, you will not be playing for long. This is usually related to the contour of the rim, and particularly to the "bite" or the degree of sharpness/roundness of the edges of the rim. A rounded rim edge is usually more comfortable. However, articulation is usually better with a sharper edge. So, one must find the right balance, an edge which is comfortable yet still enables good articulation.

The quality of the tone is the most important characteristic of the sound of the trumpet. If the tone is not rich and full, no one will want to listen no matter how skilled the trumpeter is in other areas. All other things being equal (and there are many other things), a deeper cup will produce a better tone. However, regardless of how beautiful low notes are played, the listener as well as the trumpet player will want to hear occasional high notes. And here's the problem: high notes are more difficult to play with a deeper cup. Again, there has to be a balance. One has to compromise and find a cup depth that does not noticeably sacrifice either tone or range.

While the dimensions, shape and contour of the rim and the cup are probably the most important characteristics of the mouthpiece, other elements can also be influential. For example, making the throat larger is roughly equivalent to deepening the cup. The backbore can vary from tight to open, making the tone brighter or darker and/or possibly making high notes easier or more difficult to reach.

The "trial-and-trial" approach that I advocate means just that: the player should try playing several mouthpieces in a series. A series will consist of 4-6 mouthpieces having similar, but different, characteristics. If the series is selected intelligently, there will be no errors, only trials. It will not be a matter of one mouthpiece being right and another wrong; they will all be good, and the task will be to pick the one that is the best of the series. Choosing the series "intelligently" will require some "screening," or preparatory trials of 3-4 mouthpieces having quite different characteristics. It is likely that the "screening" trials can be accomplished within a 1-2 hour session while the "series" trials may require that each mouthpiece be played for a couple of days or more before a final decision can be reached.

The "screening" trials may only succeed in determining the inside diameter of the cup that is most appropriate for the particular player. Then in the "series" trials all of the mouthpieces would have that same diameter while differing in other characteristics. Finding a good mouthpiece this way does not mean that the player may never want to, or need to, change to something else. As the player matures, and as the playing matures, the characteristics desired of a mouthpiece may change, and the search process may have to be repeated. Also, note that some internet stores will allow you to try 1-3 mouthpieces at a time on a trial basis for a week or more. So, my "trial-and-trial" approach is both feasible and affordable.

Enough with the theory, how does one sort through all the various makes of mouthpieces? I doubt anyone could provide a complete answer to this question. Although I have only sampled nine different brands, I think they are representative of the range of possibilities available. For better or worse, here are my assessments:

Bach

This is a no-brainer. Virtually everyone has played one or more Bach mouthpieces. Like most other beginners, I started with a 7C; this was when I was six years old. I switched to a Bach 6 when I was ten years old, and then to a 3C when I started playing again many years later. After playing the 3C for a year or so, I sensed that there had to be something better, and so the real search began.

Parduba

The theory behind the Parduba double cup appealed to me. A shallow cup supposedly enhanced range while the second deeper cup maintained tone quality. I tried to keep the Bach 3C cup diameter and chose the Parduba model 7. I used this piece for about six months.

A digression about cup measurements is in order here. One would think that in this space age era of high technology that measuring the dimensions of a mouthpiece would be a simple and straightforward if not trivial task. Evidently not, as one can find different charts listing remarkably different dimensions of the same mouthpieces. I am at a loss to explain this. It certainly complicates attempts to match sizes from one mouthpiece maker to another (and maybe this is why the charts differ!).

Back to the Parduba. My initial reaction was positive. Although my range did not really increase, I found it slightly easier to reach higher notes. Over time, however, a couple of things began to bother me. I realized that, compared to the Bach, it was not very comfortable and endurance became a problem, especially in long gigs. Also, my articulation seemed inferior to what it had been before.

Callet

Jerome Callet has made several important contributions to the art of trumpet playing. He has developed a novel, albeit somewhat controversial, embouchure method (which I will talk about later) and designed and manufactured some highly-acclaimed instruments (for example, the Superchops, Jazz, and Sima model trumpets). He also produced a full line of mouthpieces, and then replaced it with a new and more limited number of Superchops (SC) models. Again, trying to maintain some similarity to the Bach 3C, but wanting something shallower to enhance my high register ability, I initially ordered what I thought would be the best size, the 1S from his first line. Much to my delight and amazement, Mr. Callet called to tell me I was wrong, and that I should try the 3S. I used the 3S for about a year. It was a definite improvement over both the Bach and the Parduba. It was more comfortable than the Bach, and playing high notes was easier than with the Parduba, although there was again no increase in range. Endurance, however, was still a problem during long gigs. A couple of years later, I ordered the SC1, which was introduced with a lot of fanfare, claiming to be the best all-around mouthpiece ever produced. I was disappointed, as were many others, and the SC1 was soon replaced by the SC2 and other followers as well (the SC8 is now available).

Yamaha, Curry, Schilke

I had fleeting relationships with each of these companies' mouthpieces. I tried three pieces from each company for a few days or weeks. They were all comfortable but none improved on my range, and none, in terms of tone and articulation, were quite as good as the Callet 3S.

Asymmetrical

The Lead 342 mouthpiece, designed by a physicist (John Lynch), is a certainly a contender for the most unusual mouthpiece on the market. One side of the cup of the mouthpiece is flat, and it has to be carefully placed on the lips in a specific orientation (detailed instructions are provided). I read and was impressed by Lynch's theory behind the development of this mouthpiece. That, along with the fact that it almost guaranteed a higher range, made it irresistible. Unfortunately, it has become an interesting paperweight! Although I tried to do everything that was suggested, I could not make it work. Tone quality was dreadful and the high range in particular was screechy and unpredictable. I decided to find out if it was just me. I lent it to a trumpet colleague who had a much higher range than I did and who regularly played lead with two "big bands." He was also accustomed to using very shallow pieces so I figured he should really be able to make the Asymmetrical work. He tried it for two weeks and then, like me, gave up in frustration. I suppose it must work for some people, but it is definitely not for everyone.

GR Technologies

By my estimation, at the time I tried one, this seemed to be the hottest property on the mouthpiece circuit. GR (Gary Radke) mouthpieces usually got rave reviews on the internet bulletin boards. After corresponding with GR's sales representative (Brian Scrivner), I ordered what he and I both thought would be the best fit for me, trying to retain some similarity to the Callet 3S. I used the model 66MS for a couple of months. It has an interesting look and the plating seems to be of a slightly higher quality than that of the Callet. However, it wasn't quite as comfortable as the Callet, and the two seemed identical in terms of tone quality, articulation and range. The GR is a good piece but I don't really understand what all of the fuss is about.

Marcinkiewicz

Everything I've told you so far happened over three and a half years. Then one of my trumpet colleagues purchased a Marcinkiewicz model E14 (Bobby Shew #1). I noticed (without him saying anything) that his high notes were stronger; and he reported that his endurance was much enhanced. The E14 has a very shallow cup. I was afraid that this might impair my tone quality so I ordered an E5 (Bobby Shew #2). The result was almost instantaneous: my high notes were stronger and my endurance was improved (I used it at a long gig the day after I received it). And it got even better over the next couple of months, during which time, for the first time in two years, my range went up a full step (from high F to G). Moreover, the piece was as comfortable as the Callet and the quality of my tone was the same as well. I was hooked, but naturally I wasn't satisfied. I didn't think it was likely that I just happened to pick what was for me the best Marcinkiewicz model. So, over the following year, I tried several others, about a dozen in total. Guess what—yes, at least for a while, it turned out that the E5 was the best one for me, although others came close (for example, the E9.1 or Bobby Shew #1.5, the E12.2 or Mike Vax #1, and the standard model #10). Other models (for example, the E14 and the E10.3 or Bobby Shew 1.25) made the high range considerably easier, but not without some sacrifice in tone quality. So I used the E5 for more than a year until I discovered the E18 (Eric Miyashiro model). I had initially avoided this model because I thought the cup diameter was too small and the depth too shallow. Eventually I tried a friend's E18, and much to my amazement, it worked better than anything I had ever used; it was smaller and shallower than the E14, but yet my tone was good and my range was better than ever. This was about ten years ago and I'm still using it; and I still can't figure out exactly why it works, although I suspect the wide rim and large throat are both contributory. It should be noted that Marcinkiewicz mouthpieces are made exceptionally well; each piece is perfect, unlike some others which occasionally come with manufacturing flaws; for example, I have a Schilke, a Parduba and a Yamaha that have an abrasion, a scratch, and a plating defect, respectively. By the way, Marcinkewicz also publishes a book (*The Buzz Zone*) about embouchure development and mouthpieces. Although I can't say that I recommend it, as I found it to contain very little useful information, Marcinkiewicz's obsession with attention to detail and quality control come across loud and clear—and it shows up in his products!

Instruments

The choices for the modern trumpet player are many. There are five currently played kinds of trumpet-related instruments: the trumpet (or soprano trumpet) of course, the cornet, the flugelhorn, the piccolo trumpet, and the bass trumpet. Although all of these instruments are most commonly keyed in Bb, several other varieties are available (for example, the C trumpet, the Eb cornet, and the A piccolo trumpet); of these other keyed instruments, the C trumpet is probably the most popular (especially in France and in symphony orchestras everywhere). I have some limited experience with the piccolo and bass trumpets but none with non-Bb instruments, so I will not comment further on the latter (although I haven't ruled out playing the C soprano trumpet in the future). The Bb trumpet, cornet and flugelhorn are, together, what the vast majority of horn players play. Of the latter three instruments, the trumpet has been the primary one in use since the third or fourth decade of the 20th century. Before that the cornet was more popular; and there are two types of cornets: the short or shepherd's crook cornet and the American long cornet. The flugelhorn's popularity is quite recent, dating only from around 1960. Let's start with the trumpet.

Trumpets: vintage vs. new, student vs. professional, light vs. heavy, medium-large bore vs. large bore

Over the last 50 years, there have been major advances in the technology involved in manufacturing trumpets. Major innovations in design have also been made. The result is that we now have an amazing number of models and makes from which to choose. Furthermore, some vintage instruments, dating from the 1960's and before, have also become popular, owing to their seemingly unique characteristics. The Mt. Vernon Bach Stradivarius, the Selmer Paris K-modified, the Martin Committee, and the Conn Constellation, all from the 1950's, are probably all selling well on ebay for approximately $2000, not that much less than a comparable new model professional horn ($2400-$2800). The vintage horns, offering, for example, exceptional tone (Bach Stradivarius), flexibility (Martin Committee) or valve action (Selmer Paris), may be preferred by some players even though sometimes suffering from poor intonation compared to the newer horns manufactured with more exacting standards.

Modern trumpets come in three general levels of quality: student, intermediate and professional. Student trumpets are often simpler in design (for example, lacking a first valve slide thumb ring), may have a smaller bore, and are mass produced with minimal or no hand crafting. Intermediate horns are made to look like professional horns but have the same overall quality as student horns; most experts do not recommend them, feeling that the added cost isn't justified by the superficial enhancements. Professional trumpets are made with considerable attention to detail and each horn usually requires a substantial amount of hand crafting. The larger companies (for example, Bach and, Yamaha), and even some of the smaller companies (for example, Calicchio, Schilke), offer several models mainly differing in weight and bore (other differences may involve the copper content of the brass and the taper and size of the bell). In general, heavier trumpets produce a "darker" tone than lighter trumpets, while a larger bore produces a more "open" and "brighter" sound than a smaller bore. Most professional horns have medium-large (.459-.462") or large (.464-.470") bores. Beyond these generalizations, one has to talk about individual companies. Although I haven't tried horns from all of them, or even most of them, I think my experience will at least make the subject manageable in terms of dealing with some of the common myths.

Trumpets: Bachs, Yamahas and Other Wild Things

Bach bashing has become almost a national pastime for trumpet players, at least for the ones that frequent the internet bulletin boards. The party line is that Bach used to make great trumpets before the company moved to Indiana and was bought out by Selmer; hence the mystique associated with vintage New York and Mount Vernon Bachs persists. The design of the modern Bach Stradivarius is virtually unchanged from the original as is, allegedly, the high quality of its brass; the most popular model has always had a medium-large bore and a size 37 bell. The problem supposedly lies in quality control. It is commonly said that "no two Bachs are alike," or that "you have to try ten to find one good one." I have never seen any data supporting this view (being a scientist, I'm very fond of data). That is, to my knowledge, no one has ever conducted a study whereby a panel of experts rated ten different Bach Strads and compared them to ten instruments from another company; and, of course, the experts would have to be blindfolded when they tried the various horns so that they could not tell ahead of time which brand of instrument they were testing. My own experience is that I have only tried four of them, and they all seemed fine to me. I purchased one and have played it most of the last nineteen years. Aside from a leaky tuning slide which was easily fixed during year 3, and which can happen with any brand (read on), I have had no problem with the horn. It has that "Bach sound" (another myth maybe?) and I like it a lot. Did I just happen to find the one in ten that was good? I doubt it.

In contrast to Bach, Yamaha has a reputation for superb quality control. I have heard people say that "Yamaha is the only horn I would buy over the internet or by mail, because every Yamaha is the same." I haven't seen any controlled studies that verify that statement either, nor have I tried more than a few Yamaha horns myself. However, both the internet and my own experience testify to at least one problem that's commonly encountered with Yamaha's. The valves of some (but apparently not all) Yamaha's are sticky or slow. Curiously, the usual response to such a query on an internet bulletin board is that Yamaha makes their valves so precisely, with so little tolerance, that it takes a while (sometimes a long while) to work them in. This explanation, which I've encountered several times, turns the problem into something almost advantageous, supposedly reflecting on the high quality of Yamaha's manufacturing process. So why are the attitudes toward Bach and Yamaha so different? I really don't know but neither makes much sense. For the record, I own a Yamaha 6310Z (Bobby Shew model). This is a light horn and I prefer to use it when playing with a jazz combo. The valves were indeed very slow in the beginning—it's been almost seventeen years and they're still just a little slow compared to the faster Bach valves; but the horn is still fun to play, and flexibility, or moving from one register to another, is particularly good.

Daunting even Yamaha's reputation is a phenomenon called the Wild Thing. The Wild Thing trumpet was designed and invented by trumpeter Flip Oakes in Oceanside, California. The Wild Thing is actually made by Kanstul, but it is sold only by Flip Oakes, who also does some "enhancing" to the final product before it is shipped. Although there are probably only a few thousand at most in existence, testimonials to the merits of the Wild Thing trumpet are all over the internet bulletin boards, as well as on Flip Oakes' website. A few years ago, when the stock market began to falter and my retirement account started its long downward trend, I decided to purchase a Wild Thing trumpet. While I was excited about playing it, I primarily bought it as an investment. In view of the high resale prices of vintage instruments, and the extraordinary reputation of the Wild Thing, I figured that its value could only increase over the years; and I still think that's the case. According to the internet testimonials I read at the time, every Wild

Thing is a work of perfection, and every one is the same. I initially emailed Flip Oakes a message saying I was interested in purchasing a Wild Thing and wondered if I should order the horn unseen or come pick one out at his studio. I was planning to attend a conference in San Diego about four months later and thought I might visit Flip after the conference and bring home a Wild Thing. Flip called me at home two days later and told me that every Wild Thing was indeed the same and that there was no point in my waiting four months to have one. So, I ordered a bank transfer of the funds (as he requested) and about ten days later I received the horn.

Almost from the beginning I suspected something was wrong. The valves were unusually noisy and one of them was very sticky. I cleaned them daily, lubricated them with Blue Juice (as recommended by Flip), but to no avail. The noisiness diminished slightly while the sticky valve persisted unchanged—I couldn't get through one chorus of a tune without the valve malfunctioning. I emailed Flip about the problems, and he assured me it was just a matter of getting the lapping compound out of the horn and that over time the horn would just get better and better. Well it didn't. I also noticed that the horn had some plating defects—one could see streaks of plating on the middle of the bell as well as globs of solder or silver in a couple of places. Now keep in mind that according to the testimonials the valves were reportedly smooth and quiet, and the finish was supposedly flawless. After a month, I concluded that I had a lemon. Several email exchanges with Flip resulted in my returning the horn in exchange for a new one. Although Flip was always patient and cooperative, he found it difficult to believe that anything could be seriously wrong—he finally agreed to the exchange just to make me happy. It turned out that I was more right than I knew. Apparently, there was also something wrong with the plating on the inside of the bell—Flip even sent me a digital picture showing the defect.

The second Wild Thing arrived a couple of weeks after returning the first one. I was aghast as soon as I took it out of the case. There was a sizeable dent (with "teeth" marks appearing as if the horn had been in a vise) on the tubing going to the bell. I thought that Flip would never believe it, and that he would think I was some kind of a lunatic. I therefore took two digital pictures of the dent and emailed them to him. He was indeed shocked—supposedly both he and his wife had checked the horn before shipping. Nevertheless, he agreed to have the dent fixed and pay the shipping charges for returning it. I decided that I would play it for 2-3 months and then ship it back to him right before I was planning to be away for a couple of weeks. Fortunately, this horn indeed played the way I expected. The valves were fast and quiet; the high note slotting was excellent as were flexibility and tone.

The Wild Thing, which is a large bore (.470) instrument with an unusually large bell flare, comes with two tuning slides (#1 and #2). Slide #1 maintains the same bore and produces the most open sound. Slide #2 has a tapered smaller bore and produces a darker and richer sound. Flip also offered the option of purchasing two in-between slides (#3 and #4), so you could have essentially four horns in one. I figured I might as well go for the whole package, and I quickly purchased both of the additional slides. Over the next two months I discovered that two of the tuning slides (#2 and #3) were leaky. Hence, when I returned the horn for repair, I sent back both of the latter slides for Flip to fix. Flip fixed both of the slides and then sent the horn to the Kanstul factory for repair of the dent. The repaired horn came back to me about a month later. I opened up the case with trepidation and, although it wasn't my worst fear, there was in fact a problem. The #3 slide was crimped on the end, apparently damaged (mishandled) in the factory. At that point I just didn't want to deal with returning anything to anyone, although I did inform Flip about the damaged slide. So I attempted to fix it myself with the conical end of a paintbrush handle—more than a year later I improved upon this with a special Feree tool. Although my fix of the slide looks pretty good, frankly I've been afraid to use it and never have.

The simple moral to my Wild Thing story is that nothing is perfect. Conversely, I suspect that most of the Bach bashing is unwarranted. There are just many more Bachs out there than Wild Things so naturally you're going to hear many more complaints about the former than the latter. An obvious corollary is that, if at all possible, it is preferable to see and try a horn before purchasing it. However, for many of us, this is not possible; for example, a Bach is about the only brand of professional horn you could buy at a store in the Albany, NY area. Thus one needs to be especially astute and patient, carefully testing a new horn and returning it if not satisfied. If something appears to be wrong, it probably is wrong; that is, don't let someone easily convince you otherwise.

Now what about all of the other brands of professional horns that I haven't tried extensively? Although I can't comment at length, I have had some experience with a few other horns and talked to others who have used them. I've played a Calicchio (Studio 2 model) and a "New French" Besson. The Besson seemed very similar to my Bach Strad and the Calicchio seemed very similar to my Yamaha 6310Z. I've heard uniform praise for Schilke horns (several models) as well as for the Callet Jazz model. Schilke models as well as the Callet Jazz and the Yamaha 6310Z have a variable or progressive bore, starting small and becoming large as the tubing approaches the bell. This seems to enhance flexibility. Eventually, about four years after the Wild Thing saga, I bought a used Schilke, model B5. This confirmed everything good I'd heard about Schilkes—excellent intonation and flexibility, flawless valves and slides.

Representing perhaps the two extremes of trumpets, at least in terms of cost, are Jupiter and Monette; some readers may be appalled by my even mentioning both in the same sentence. Jupiter's are made in Korea and have steadily improved over the years. I've tried a few and, for the cost, they're not bad. In fact, I own a Jupiter pocket trumpet (now about $750) that I take with me whenever I travel; and I even played a gig with it once. The only problem I've noticed in all of the Jupiter's I've tried is that intonation is a little off in the high register. With regard to Monette instruments, unfortunately I've never had the pleasure. Made in Oregon by Dave Monette, they sell for upwards of $10,000 and I've never seen or heard anyone other than a well known professional use one; their mouthpieces, which are sometimes used by amateurs like me, sell for about $200. Although internet testimonials attest to the uniqueness and superior craftsmanship of the Monette instruments, curiously one occasionally sees some bashing of Monette mouthpieces. Nothing is sacred on the internet.

Lastly, let's briefly return to vintage trumpets again. Okay, I have one of these too; well maybe two. That is, the first is my original Conn 22B (New York Symphony model, made in 1953)—my parents bought it new for me in 1955; I think it cost about $130. I played the 22B for ten years, the whole time I was growing up and taking lessons. Let's just say that it doesn't hold a candle to my Bach Strad. Now the real vintage professional horn that I own is a Selmer K-modified, made in 1959. I bought it from Rich Ita (www.brassinstrumentworkshop.com). By the way, he is a terrific guy who won't let you keep anything unless you really like it. The Selmer K-modified was a popular jazz horn in the 50's and 60's and, after reading everything I could find about it, I searched for one for about a year. Rich Ita said the one I bought is one of the best K-modified's he's ever played—and I believe him. It has a dark, unusual tone (hard to describe)—I especially like playing it with the lights out. Obviously, if you're intent on purchasing a vintage (very old) horn, it's generally even riskier, sight unseen, than purchasing a new horn. However, if you deal with Rich Ita, the risk is probably zero or close to it.

Cornets

Compared to the trumpet and even the flugelhorn, the cornet is currently a neglected and overlooked instrument. Why this is the case is entirely unclear to me inasmuch as a century ago the cornet reigned supreme. In some ways, the cornet is a much more interesting instrument than the trumpet. While trumpets differ in bore and bell size, the basic design has remained pretty much the same over the years. In contrast, cornet designs have varied enormously. The quickest way to be convinced of this is to visit a couple of internet sites that sell vintage and contemporary cornets. Look at the pictures of cornets at Rich Ita's Brass Instrument Workshop (cited above) as well as those at Steve Dillard's site (www.horntrader.com).

In general, the cornet has a mellower tone than the trumpet. As noted earlier, there are two general types of cornets, the short or shepherd's crook cornet and the American long cornet. The short cornet originated first, circa 1835, while the long cornet became more popular 90-100 years later. The short cornet sounds mellower than the long cornet, the latter sounding more similar to the trumpet. The smaller size of the cornet, both types being smaller than the trumpet, provides at least one advantage compared to the trumpet: it's somewhat easier to deal with mutes, particularly manipulations involving the use of the plunger mute. The softer sound can also be much more appealing in particular settings. When playing with my jazz quintet, there are some tunes that definitely sounded better with the cornet than with the trumpet.

Although I haven't tried many cornets, there are three that I play periodically, and three others that, based on reputation, I would certainly like to play. The one I use most is a Yamaha light model (6330S). Although the tone is not as dark as some cornets, it is a very versatile instrument, easy to play with good intonation in the high register. In my experience, poor intonation can be a major problem with some cornets. In addition to the Yamaha, I have two vintage cornets: a Schenkelaars (made in the Netherlands) long model (a circa 1945 copy of the Conn Constellation, purchased privately online) and a Besson (made in England) short model (circa 1900, purchased from Rich Ita). Both are fun to play, the Schenkelaars having an open, almost trumpet-like sound and the Besson having a dark, mellow, lyrical sound. Regarding other contemporary models, Schilke (model XA1) and Besson (Sovereign) both make highly rated cornets that someday I would love to play. However, the cornet I'm most eager to play is the Marcinkiewicz Rembrandt. I've corresponded with several people who have one—all gave it rave reviews; and if Marcinkiewicz takes the same care in the manufacture of his instruments as he does with his mouthpieces, the result must be remarkable indeed.

Flugelhorns

Many modern jazz trumpeters now also play the flugelhorn—it's almost becoming the norm. Although I've had a flugelhorn for many years, I only started playing it regularly with my trio about a year ago. I use it primarily on slow ballads, where its blending with the guitar and bass sounds especially good. I use a Yamaha 6310Z (Bobby Shew model)—it sounds far superior to two cheaper (and larger bore) models I've tried (Jupiter and Getzen). The small bore of the Yamaha 6310Z is reputedly a throwback to the early Couesnon models of the last century. Yamaha makes larger bore models too but I have no intention of switching. A somewhat more expensive flugelhorn is the Kanstul model 1525. I've played one several times, and if I was going to switch to a larger bore, this would be the horn I would buy. It has an exceptionally sweet tone.

Footnote: the pocket trumpet

The first time I saw and heard a pocket trumpet I was simply amazed. How could something so small produce the sound of a full-sized trumpet (well almost!)! Although Don Cherry played the pocket trumpet as his main instrument, most people (myself included) consider it a travel instrument. As I noted earlier, I take it with me whenever I go anywhere overnight. Although pocket trumpets are made by several companies and can be as expensive as full-sized trumpets, my advice is to get the cheapest one you can find. If you're in a hotel room, you will have to use a practice mute anyway, so even an expensive instrument is not going to sound great. My view is that it's great just to have something to play when away from home.

Mutes

Mutes come in a variety of shapes, are made of a variety of materials, and produce a variety of different sounds; and I'm limiting this topic to just trumpet/cornet mutes. The most commonly used mute is the straight mute; in order of popularity, the cup mute, the Harmon (wah-wah) mute, and the plunger mute are probably next. Then there is the bucket mute, as well as some rarely used mutes, for example, the derby (hat), the solotone, and the purdie. And of course, there are soft-sounding practice mutes. Lastly, there are some felt and foam creations that produce sounds all their own.

Straight and cup mutes

I'm considering straight and cup mutes together because most straight mutes have cup mute cousins made the same way and also because sometimes cup and straight mutes are incorporated in the same mute; that is, the cup is detachable. I'm not really certain of this (I haven't seen any data), but I suspect that the most popular cup and straight mutes are the inexpensive (less than $30) stonelined mutes made by Humes & Berg. They seem to be ubiquitous. However, personally, I'm not fond of their sound, which I think borders on harsh. Plastic (polyethylene) mutes (for example, Bach) cost about the same and sound better to me; an especially good black polymer straight mute is made by Mutec (model MHT110). But metal (aluminum) cup and straight mutes, preferably with copper bottoms (producing a darker sound), are probably the best, having the most consistent intonation across registers. The Jo-Ral cup and straight mutes are particularly good; and a unique feature of all Jo-Ral mutes is that the corks are rubberized, producing a better fit to the horn and lasting longer than ordinary cork. The Jo-Ral cup mute (called the Tri-Tone) also comes with felt inserts that can substantially soften the tone.

A straight mute made of wood in Germany was introduced a few years ago. This mute, made by Amrein, seems to have a softer sound and even better intonation than metal mutes; however, it's a bit pricey (about $125) as well as delicate—it's very light and could easily be damaged. A relatively new and extensive line of wooden mutes is now produced by Facet Mutes, Inc. Different kinds of wood are used to make several different varieties of both straight and cup mutes. I haven't played any of them but the recordings I've heard sound very good, and I'm tempted to buy one. However, I'm resisting for now as these mutes are probably the most expensive ($150-$200) of all.

Several cup mutes come with detachable/adjustable cups. This allows one to soften and dampen the usual cup mute sound as well as take off the cup entirely and use the remaining piece as a straight mute. There are at least three excellent versions of this design, one made by Dennis Wick, another by Yamaha, and another by Mutec. And Harmon makes one (the "Triple Play Combo") that is definitively inferior; the cup attaches in an imprecise way and the intonation (in either cup or straight configuration) borders on horrible.

Wah-wah mutes: "Harmon" and bubble

Harmon invented the wah-wah mute (which it now calls the "Wow-Wow") and, when indicated on music, the "Harmon mute" generally refers to any mute producing the wah-wah sound. With at least one exception, they all have a detachable inner cup; in fact, the Harmon mute is more commonly played without the inner cup. My own experience is that the quality of the Harmon company's mutes has declined substantially over the last 50-60 years. I have an old Harmon mute, made by Harmon in 1957-58, and a much newer Harmon-made Harmon mute that I bought in 1998. The metal of the old one is about twice as thick as the metal of the new one, and the old one sounds better too, although it needs to have its cork replaced. I no longer use the new one—it fell out of my trumpet a couple of years ago and was severely damaged; and note that the old one has fallen out several times and sustained only very minimal damage. Mutec makes an excellent Harmon mute that has the sound and durability of the old Harmon-made Harmon mute.

A modern variation on the Harmon mute is the Jo-Ral Bubble mute. The bubble mute produces a softer sound than the Harmon and the two can be used interchangeably. Personally, however, I prefer a copper Harmon mute. Mutec makes an excellent one—I think the sound is even better than the bubble and the shape of the mute makes it easier to handle than the bubble. Walt Johnson sells a soft-sounding fiberglass Harmon-like mute that lacks an inner cup. It's called the Miles Mute; the design seems to have been inspired by Miles Davis, who often played a Harmon without the cup inserted. Lastly, and mainly of historical interest, Bobby Shew once designed and sold a copper mute also resembling a Harmon mute without the inner cup. Because I have a fondness for anything Bobby Shew designs, I ordered this mute and was quite excited when it arrived. Although it really looked beautiful (or as beautiful as a mute can look), I was quickly disappointed. It would simply not stay in the trumpet for more than 30 seconds; and I tried huffing (blowing warm air) on the bell to no avail. The amount of cork in contact with the bell was relatively meager, reflecting I think, a design defect. The store that sold it to me did not agree with my analysis of the problem (or that there was a problem) but agreed to take it back. Eventually, Bobby Shew stopped having it made. C'est la vie—even Bobby Shew isn't perfect.

Plungers and plunger mutes

The plunger mute has a long history of creative use, starting with Ellington's trumpeters (Bubber Miley, Buck Clayton) in the 1930's and 1940'and continuing to the present (Wynton Marsalis). Although a few companies (Jo-Ral, Dennis Wick, Humes & Berg) sell plunger mutes, I've rarely seen anyone use one of these. Everyone seems to use the real thing—a plunger (that is, the rubber end of a plunger). Plungers come in different sizes, intended for different purposes (floor drain vs. sink drain vs. a toilet). While many trumpeters use a 5-inch (diameter) plunger, a 4-inch plunger (intended for sink drains) is really the best size to use. Not only does the smaller size sound better, because it's not totally covering the bell, but it's also much easier to manipulate, thereby enhancing your ability to create strange and wonderful effects. However, the 4-inch sized plunger can be hard to find. None of my local hardware or grocery stores carried it, and I finally ordered a few ($2.00 each) from an internet store.

Practice mutes

A practice mute is intended to mute your sound to the extent that no one in the next room will hear you. Having one of these is almost mandatory if you want to practice while you're staying in a hotel. The top of the line in practice mutes is the one that comes with Yamaha's Silent Brass system. And if you also use the electronic part of this system (including earphones), you can hear yourself loud and clear, even with special effects (reverberation). Other practice mutes don't dampen the sound as much as Yamaha's but do produce a nicer sound in the absence of an electronic hookup; in addition to allowing you to practice in a quiet environment, these other mutes can occasionally be used to produce a nice effect in a combo setting. I personally recommend the Jo-Ral practice mute for this purpose.

Bucket mutes

There are two basic kinds of bucket mutes: ones that clip on the bell and ones that go in the bell like a straight or cup mute would. Probably the most popular clip-on bucket mute is the stonelined one made by Humes & Berg while the Jo-Ral bucket, made of aluminum (with or without a copper bottom), is probably the best of the in-bell kind. I prefer the clip-on mute because it has a much softer sound than in the in-bell mute; and the former costs much less than the latter ($30 vs. $60). A black plastic clip-on bucket mute, called the EaZy Bucket ($40), became available a few years ago; it's sturdier, easier to take on and off, and sounds nearly identical to the Humes & Berg mute.

Solotone, purdie, and derby

The solotone mute looks like two straight mutes on top of each other. And, to me, the sound of it resembles what I would expect of doubling the effect of a straight mute. The purdie mute, which attaches to the rim of the bell, looks like a metal circular plate with a hole in the center. It's supposed to make the trumpet sound more like a flugelhorn—in my opinion, it doesn't come close. The derby, looking like a hat, was popular in the 1930's. These days, when an arrangement calls for a "hat," you usually put your bell very close (2-3 inches away) to your music—it produces a similar effect but is much simpler to do.

Bags, foam and other muting devices

Velvet bags, including ones that used to hold bottles of whisky, are sometimes used as mutes. Some are even sold as mutes. The effect is a slightly softer sound—nice and gentle and most appropriate for playing slow ballads in dim lights. Another way of softening the sound is to use foam rubber, either as an insert into a cup mute, a rim around a straight mute, or by itself. The Softone mute is essentially all foam rubber encased in a soft neoprene shell—you can remove one or more layers of foam and produce a variety of effects. Lastly, my wife and I have invented a felt mute that we call the Trugel mute. It's made of several layers of felt sewn together, and easily slips on and off the bell. The Trugel mute produces a sound resembling that of a flugelhorn; or at least the resemblance is closer than that of any other mute I've tried. I use it when I don't want to bother taking the flugelhorn with me.

Valve oils and slide greases

The search for the perfect valve oil seems endless, and new ones are continuing to be created. The perfect oil would be a superior lubricant (enabling the valves to move with lightening speed), last forever (or at least for a week), include a disinfectant (that would also suppress mold formation), and be safe and environmentally "friendly" (no petroleum distillates); and, although there is some disagreement about this, I think it should also be odorless. After trying about a dozen of the more popular oils, I've concluded that it's impossible to generalize; that is, no one oil is the best for all horns and for all purposes. Now I will try to describe how I came to this conclusion.

I haven't seen any sales figures but, based on the numerous comments I've read on the trumpet bulletin boards, I suspect that Al Cass is the best selling valve oil. It seems to be the benchmark to which every other oil is compared. Personally, for the most part, I think this status is well deserved. Al Cass is indeed an excellent lubricant and, with a couple of exceptions I will get to later, I haven't found another oil that allows valves to move as fast or faster. It's also odorless. However, like most other valve oils, it's a petroleum distillate and, as far as I know, it contains no disinfectant. It does not last very long either—applying it before or after each daily practice session is best. My experience is that it works best on modern and more expensive valves (made of Monel) having minimal clearances. For example, I used to use it routinely with my Bach Strad and Yamaha 6310Z, but it does not work very well in my Jupiter pocket trumpet or my circa 1900 Besson cornet; the valves seem "sticky" when used in both of the latter instruments. But overall, for most modern "professional" horns, the Al Cass oil is certainly a contender for one of the better lubricants.

Zaja valve oils, and there are several, come with different fragrances (for example, strawberry, watermelon, lemon, and even swiss chocolate) although there is also an odorless variety, Zaja Blue. Comments on the internet testify to Zaja's excellent lubricating properties as well as to the desirability of one fragrance or another. I bought and tested the one with a mulberry fragrance. The oil worked well, almost but not quite as well as Al Cass. However, I only tested it for a couple of weeks because I developed a strong aversion to the odor. It was disconcerting to be able to smell my trumpet before I even picked it up. It's a mystery to me as to why some people like their valve oil to have an odor.

Blue Juice, which has a disinfectant in it, is fast but not as fast as Al Cass. It's odorless and seems to leave the valves looking a little cleaner. Flip Oakes ("Wild Thing" inventer) recommends using it to help get the lapping compound out of a new horn. I don't know why this happens but I've noticed that after I use it repeatedly for several days the valves start to get a little sticky; and I've repeated this experiment several times.

I now use it once in a while in a couple of horns—I apply it after a practice session and usually when I know I'm not going to use that particular horn for at least 2-3 days.

Binak 495 is the oil that is perhaps most different from all others. It's supposedly very safe (no petroleum distillates), contains an anti-corrosive that protects the horn, lasts for a long time, and has only a slight unobjectionable odor; and it takes only 2-3 drops of the oil to lubricate a valve. The downside is that it's not very fast; in fact, if you apply too much, it's even slower (I learned this the hard way). I've found that it works best on relatively loose valves—for example, my Jupiter pocket trumpet and 1900 Besson cornet. It's also a great "storage" oil; that is, if you know you're not going to play a horn for several days or weeks, using Binak 495 will prevent the valves from locking up, which can easily happen with other oils. Eventually, to combat the slowness problem, the same company introduced Binak Pro. The latter is thinner than its predecessor and is claimed to enable exceptionally fast valve action. I've tested the Pro version in several horns, and my impression is that the new oil is just a little faster—not a huge advance, but welcome nonetheless. Interestingly, it works extremely well in my Wild Thing.

Hetman produces what might be considered the Cadillacs of valve/slide oils and greases—well at least with regard to price (with one exception, they are probably the most expensive). I've tried two Hetman valve oils (and two slide greases that I will get to later)—piston lubricants 2 and 3. To me, the #2 seems very similar to Al Cass—as far as I can tell, they work equally well. The #3 is also called the "classic" and is intended for relatively loose fitting valves, as often found in old, "classic" instruments. I've only tried it in my 1900 Besson cornet, and it works very well, considerably faster than Binak 495—it's now the only oil I use for that cornet.

Ultra-Pure Professional Valve Oil, made of synthetic oils, is non-toxic and odorless. I started to use it only a couple of years ago, after I saw an endorsement by Wynton Marsalis. It's not the fastest oil but it's very smooth; the valves almost seem to slide up and down by themselves. It works especially well in my Bach Stradivarius. I'm not sure why that's the case, but I now use it routinely for that instrument.

Probably the most expensive valve oil on the U.S. market is La Tromba T2 Valve Oil Special. It's made in Switzerland and is very fast and long-lasting. I discovered it three or four years ago and now use it regularly in my Yamaha 6310Z trumpet. I also use it occasionally in other horns when the valves don't seem to be as quick as they used to be; the T2 oil fixes the problem and then I can return to using whichever cheaper oil I was using in that horn. I suspect this may be the best valve oil ever invented, and if the price comes down a bit, I may start to use it routinely in all of my horns.

Any review of valve oils would be remiss if Holton was not mentioned. This is the oil that most of us comeback players probably used when growing up. In fact, as far as I knew when I was ten or fifteen years old, it was the only oil, or at least the only oil that my local music store stocked. The formula for the Holton oil has supposedly not changed over the years, although I'm not sure if this is really true. In any case, it still works decently, mixing with water (saliva) better than most others. The one objectionable feature is that it has a somewhat obnoxious odor—and for that reason alone, I no longer use it.

The Brass Spa's H$_2$OIL Valve Oil is claimed to be both fast and long-acting, the "best on the planet." It is also odorless and mixes well with water. However, it's not faster than Al Cass—at least in my instruments, it's a little slower. Also, although I have found it to be long-lasting, I've noticed that over the course of a week, some residue accumulates on the valves, eventually making them sticky. If you clean and lubricate the valves every 2-3 days this is not a problem.

Yamaha and Bach both make decent valve oils that are similar to each other. Both are reasonably fast (but not quite as fast as Al Cass) and have negligible odors. Both the Yamaha and Bach oils seem to last a little longer than Al Cass.

The last oil to be mentioned is not in fact sold as a valve oil. I'm referring to unscented lamp oil, commonly sold as fuel for oil lamps. There's a bit of controversy about whether or not lamp oil can do any harm to instruments; as far as I can tell, there are no compelling data that support either point of view. However, one thing is certain: lamp oil can function as an amazingly fast valve oil. Although I've only tried it a few times, due to the fear of the unknown regarding the possibility of damage, it's truly faster than any of the valve oils I've mentioned; it's also cheaper than any valve oil. But it doesn't last long—if I were brave enough to use it on a long-term basis, daily application would be mandatory.

Now let's turn our attention to slide greases. There are only a few that are worth mentioning. Before doing so however, it should be noted that many valve oils claim to be useful as slide lubricants as well. I don't recommend this. In my experience, a slide treated with valve oil moves either too fast or erratically and is difficult to control (for example, when extending first or third valve slides). In my opinion, the best slide grease for routine use is Schilke slide grease. It's neither too thin nor too thick and lasts a long time; the slides move smoothly and are easy to control. Selmer makes a "cork and slide grease" that's not bad as a back-up; it's a little thinner than the Schilke grease and might be preferable if you have a very tight-fitting slide. At the other extreme, for loose fitting slides, Hetman makes a slide grease that's a little thicker than the Schilke grease. Hetman also makes an "ultra" slide grease that feels less like grease and more like chewing gum; that is, it's very sticky. The "ultra" may be useful for exceptionally loose-fitting slides; in fact, it's probably most useful on a loose-fitting second valve slide, because it doesn't have to move while you're playing.

Miscellaneous accessories and treatments

Although I haven't seen any sales data, several authorities have made comments suggesting that trumpet players love gimmicks and will purchase anything costing less than $50. There are an astounding number of such accessories available and, because I haven't tried them, I won't comment on most of them. However, I've had some experience with a few.

Heavy valve caps

I routinely use Bach heavy valve caps on my Bach Strad. Is there any difference in the sound? None that I can discern. I only use them because they are easier to remove and replace than the ordinary ones that came with the instrument. But the Bach heavy caps are only twice as heavy as the originals. I have no idea how the monster-sized caps made by Reeves and others would affect the sound of the horn. And of course, I've never heard of a controlled experiment being done to find out.

Heavy mouthpieces

I have two of these—the heavy version of a Bach 3C and the heavy version of a Marcinkiewicz E5 (Bobby Shew #2). Again, there are no objective data here, but my impression is that the heavy pieces darken the tone in a nice way. I've mainly used the heavy E5 on my Wild Thing trumpet and the heavy 3C on my 1900 Besson cornet. For those who are interested in learning more about the theory behind making heavy pieces, I refer you to Marcinkiewicz's book, *The Buzz Zone*.

Brass valve guides and fast springs

For unknown reasons (probably cost), Bach, Yamaha and Schilke replaced brass valve guides with plastic guides in some or most of their instruments. Supposedly (according to a sales pitch), just replacing a third valve plastic guide with a brass guide will improve the tone of the instrument. I tried this with my Bach Strad (which came with plastic guides); detecting no difference whatsoever, I replaced the plastic guide. The valves of my Yamaha 6310Z trumpet have always been a little slow, so I tried replacing the springs with special springs guaranteed to be super fast. The new springs were noisier but not faster, so I replaced the original springs. This topic should probably be explored more fully if I ever write a second edition.

Digital valve alignment

I own two instruments that came with digitally aligned valves. Their valves work very well. However, the valves of my Bach Strad, which came with factory aligned valves, work equally well, or maybe even slightly better. My own experience is that, with new instruments, the valves continually improve with use for about the first two years, depending of course on how regularly the instrument is played. Even the relatively slow valves of my Yamaha 6310Z have improved substantially; and, even without a digital valve alignment, I suspect they will eventually catch up to the Bach Strad. I think valves eventually align themselves, and the digital valve alignment is a way of dramatically hastening the process. Whether you decide to have it done or not may depend on how patient you are. Of course, if the valves are really defective, that's another story.

Cryogenic treatment

Cooling a brass instrument down to -300°F or less supposedly alters the metal in a way that mimics 30 years of aging. The process purportedly reduces "stress" and "tension" in the metal, improving the instrument's intonation. The proponents of this process claim that the instrument "feels" different although exactly how is difficult to describe. I don't know who conceived of this process but there used to be at least a half dozen places where you could have it done; my impression is that its popularity and availability have waned in recent years. A couple of experiments have been conducted to determine if trumpets differed before and after cryogenic treatment. The results were mixed, although one thing that was clear was that cryogenic treatment had no effect on the physical characteristics of the sound produced. However, in playing tests involving four trumpeters and three trumpets, cryogenic treatment generally improved the playing characteristics of the instruments. But the data were not subjected to any kind of statistical analysis, so it is impossible to be certain that the instruments were really affected by the process. In a subsequent and larger experiment involving six trumpeters and ten trumpets, the differences were minimal and statistically insignificant. Perhaps an even larger experiment is merited. In the meantime, I think one's money is better spent elsewhere.

Cleaning (mouthpiece and leadpipe)

There is ample advice available elsewhere regarding the details of how to clean and take care of instruments. The only point I would like to make here is that the closer you get to the mouth the quicker that part of the instrument becomes dirty. The mouthpiece should be rinsed after each playing/practice session, and it should be cleaned more thoroughly on a weekly basis. While a mouthpiece brush is obviously helpful, I've found that a cotton tipped applicator is particularly useful for cleaning the throat, which can easily be scratched by a mouthpiece brush. Next in importance is the leadpipe, which will usually contain more "sludge" than the rest of the instrument in total. The simplest, quickest and most effective way to clean the leadpipe is to use a leadpipe swab; pulling the swab through the leadpipe 3-5 times takes less than five minutes. Depending on the extent of your prior negligence, cleaning the leadpipe can produce a very noticeable improvement in your tone quality. My recommendation is to do it at least once for every 30 hours of playing.

Lastly in this section, I'd like to note that many years ago I discovered a somewhat unusual and excellent resource for cleaning my instruments. Kimwipes, made by Kimberly-Clark, are widely used in laboratories everywhere. However, they are also very useful in cleaning mouthpieces and valves, and even the end of the leadpipe. They leave virtually no lint and are very absorbent. They work so well that I once wrote a letter to the company suggesting that they re-package them and sell them as "music wipes." They ignored my suggestion, but fortunately the wipes are available from many online sites (including Amazon).

PART II: TECHNICAL ASPECTS OF PLAYING

I haven't counted but I would guess there are in excess of 100 books that deal with basic methods and techniques of playing the trumpet. Many if not most of these include extensive series of exercises to accomplish one goal or another (for example, developing flexibility, reaching high notes etc.). The Arban book is still the ultimate reference in this regard. I have no intention of attempting to compete with any of these more authoritative sources, not that I would have a chance of succeeding. Keep in mind that I'm an amateur talking to amateurs. My sole intention is to make recommendations that, based on my own experience, are practical, in terms of time and commitment, and effective, in terms of being able to play decently. In my opinion one of the best books published on this topic is *Brass Tactics* by Chase Sanborn. Mr. Sanborn, who is a very accomplished jazz trumpet player himself, covers just about everything anyone would want to know; and he does so with a sense of clarity (and humor) missing in other texts. However, he, like every other trumpeter author I've read, implicitly assumes that the reader aspires to be a professional and/or has the time to learn to play like a professional. He can't help it—he's a professional! On the other hand my expectations are considerably less (more realistic, I think). If you're still reading this book, then your aspirations are to learn to play as well as you can with a limited amount of daily practice time (two hours maximum).

Embouchure

To paraphrase the advice Mr. Arban gave more than a hundred years ago, what feels best for you is probably best for you. Everyone's mouth is different and it's unreasonable to expect that the interface between mouthpiece and lips will be exactly the same for any two people. The usual advice is to have the mouthpiece placed one-third on the top lip and two-thirds on the bottom lip. Beyond that, things get complicated and controversial.

These days the discussion of embouchure is intertwined with the quest for playing higher and higher notes. Everyone is looking for a shortcut, a magical solution, or even a longer program of study as long as it will guarantee that presently unattainable notes will eventually be reached. To satisfy this desire (that is, to take advantage of the sizeable market), several methods and programs in fact make the promises that everyone wants to hear. I've tried a few of them myself, enough to conclude that miraculous high notes don't happen. I will recount my experiences with five representative approaches.

Double High C in 37 weeks (by Roger W. Spaulding), as the name implies, is no shortcut. It's a 37-week course of exercises. The essence of the course is pedal tones, notes going as low as an octave and a half below low F#, the lowest "ordinary" note of the trumpet. The basic premise is that playing pedal tones will somehow prepare you for being able to play the high register leading to double high C. The 37-week program entails going through the book twice, but practicing only on alternate days. That is, optimally, according to the instructions, one would only play the trumpet on alternate days and only play the exercises in the book that are scheduled for that particular day. However, the author acknowledges that this regimen is probably not possible for most people. Nevertheless, the book requires patience and diligence. Since I thought I was capable of both, I decided to try this program. After some initial difficulties, I managed to do pretty well with producing pedal tones. Aside from being able to play the note, the major problem at first was figuring out what the note was, since I wasn't used to looking at notes that far below the staff. Eventually the exercises start going higher and higher, and that's when frustration set in. At the time I started this program, my highest note was high E. When the exercises went higher than high E, I simply couldn't play them. But I persisted and continued the program, playing as much of the exercises as I could and trying as hard as I could to reach all of the notes prescribed for each day. I persisted for close to 30 weeks and then, realizing my highest high note was still high E, I gave up, deciding that my time would be better spent learning to play music.

Superchops by Jerry Callet is primarily an embouchure method, one of several that have been advanced over the years (the methods of Farkas and Stevens are others). Callet apparently based his method on an analysis of how some of the most famous professionals reached high notes. The essential characteristics of the Superchops embouchure are that the bottom lip is brought up over the top teeth as higher notes are played and tonguing is aimed straight between the teeth, not in back of the front teeth; and the tongue is kept straight with no arching. Rather than being in a "smile" or "pucker" formation, the lips are "drawn inward" by the "bunching upwards of the chin" to create a cushion. In addition to a short book, Callet originally sold a videotape illustrating his method. Surprisingly, I found the book to be much more useful than the videotape. The method, although at odds with more common recommendations (for example, tonguing to the back of the front teeth), is really quite simple. I conscientiously worked on the Superchops method for a couple of months, and my range did indeed increase a half step (to high F); also, I began to have less difficulty reaching my highest notes on a regular basis. It's hard to say whether the Superchops method was really responsible for this improvement since my range now (up to high G) is the same whether I use the Superchops embouchure or not. I tend to think that just working on the method opened my throat a little and improved my air flow.

Double High C in Ten Minutes by Walt Johnson, a trumpeter who makes and sells a popular line of instrument cases, is perhaps the antithesis to both of the approaches above. Johnson advocates using one embouchure for low and mid-range notes and another "high gear" embouchure for high notes. The latter involves simply rolling the lips in a little. This may work for him but it was certainly of little consequence for me; and I found it awkward to try changing my embouchure while playing. If something sounds too good to be true (like the title of the book), it probably isn't true. I think Johnson should stick to making his cases.

Chop-Sticks is not a book and, in this context, has nothing to do with eating Asian food. It entails the use of five steel rods in a series of exercises designed to strengthen the lip and thereby enhance range. It's been trumpet folklore for years that holding a pencil (eraser end) between your lips for 10-60 seconds a day will make it easier to reach high notes. If this has a benefit (which has never been proven), it probably occurs early in the course of learning to play, at a time when the lips are beginning to get stronger. Nevertheless, this didn't discourage someone from capitalizing on the possibility that such an activity might be helpful for everyone. The Chop-Sticks, available from www.liemartech.com, come in a mouthpiece-sized pouch along with detailed instructions on how to conduct the recommended daily exercises. The Chop-Sticks, each 3 to 3 ½ inches long and covered in plastic/rubber for an inch at one end, vary in diameter and weight. The exercises involve a lot more than just simply holding each of the Chop-Sticks between your lips; the instructions have you trying to twist them with your lips in various ways. After two months of trying (largely unsuccessfully) to comply with the demands of the program, I gave up. I have my doubts that some of the exercises are doable by anyone. Perhaps needless to say, my playing ability was not altered in the slightest.

The Tasteebros Way, by Scott Englebright and Donny Dyess, is a book that is mainly about breathing correctly. The authors had a strange website (tasteebros.com; and calling it strange is an understatement), which is quite different now; so when I ordered their book I didn't expect much—I thought it would be more amusing than useful. Fortunately, I was wrong. The book is entirely "straight" and filled with helpful suggestions and advice. The authors believe (and I tend to agree with them) that correct breathing is the key to the high register. According to them, other than having strong corners of the mouth (to support a high velocity of air flow), what particular embouchure is used is relatively unimportant. The Tasteebros make amazingly simple, logical, and practical recommendations to help you maximize your use of air and involve the abdominal muscles as much as possible. Personally, next to learning to breathe with the abdomen, learning to keep my throat open has had the largest effect. Just making a quick silent yawn (opening the throat) prior to inhaling enhances my ability to play high notes. I think *The Tasteebros Way* is largely responsible for my highest note advancing a step (from high F to G), and more importantly, for my having a stronger and more consistent high register in general. A nice adjunct to the *The Tasteebros Way* was a cassette tape called *Complete Breathing* by Rich Szabo, another high note specialist. The tape came with an A*ir Extender*, which is a plastic tube; breathing through the tube supposedly opens your throat and increases your lung capacity. Although I was unimpressed with the tube (yawning was quicker and seemed to have the same effect), the tape was quite instructive in helping me to learn how to inhale completely and make maximal use of my breath.

Okay, if you have been paying attention, you've probably noticed that I've twice given credit for my improved high range. In addition to learning to breathe correctly, as just noted, I earlier attributed the advance in my high range to the Marcinkiewicz E5 mouthpiece. The truth is that, although the two things happened at about the same time, there was enough time between them to credit both of them. That is, I read the *The Tasteebros Way* (and listened to the Rich Szabo tape too) a couple of weeks after I switched to the Marcinkiewicz E5 mouthpiece. As described earlier, the mouthpiece itself had an immediate effect—but the effect was not fully realized until my breathing improved. While the mouthpiece was clearly the right tool for the job, correct breathing allowed me to make optimal use of the tool.

Lastly, before we close our discussion of embouchure topics, some mention should be made about two common lip exercises. I'm referring to buzzing and flapping. Buzzing occurs when we place our lips and blow as if we're going to play the trumpet—except that no trumpet is connected to our lips. Buzzing can be done with or without a mouthpiece, and there are "aids" that let you attach your mouthpiece to the leadpipe of your trumpet in a way that does not allow the air to go through the leadpipe; this lets you go through the motions of pressing the valves while buzzing outside of the trumpet and making much less noise. Many people maintain that buzzing is both great for the lips and for intonation. That is, with or without a mouthpiece, you can learn to buzz a couple of octaves. Since there are no valves to help, the note is produced only by your memory of how the note is supposed to sound. By doing this often, and occasionally checking the accuracy of your intonation, your conception of the tone will become stronger. There is some controversy as to whether buzzing is better done with or without the mouthpiece. Either way of course, buzzing may be good for keeping your lips strong. So does buzzing really do what it's supposed to do? Unfortunately, I know of no published data that prove or disprove its benefits. I've done quite a bit of buzzing myself, both with and without the mouthpiece. Although I feel virtuous when I do it, I really can't say that it accomplishes anything.

Now flapping, in my opinion, is entirely different. While buzzing requires that the lips be tense, flapping occurs when the lips are totally relaxed and allowed to vibrate without making any sound (at least not musical) other than, perhaps, that of a horse doing a similar thing. Flapping requires little effort and feels good, almost as if the lips are being massaged. Although again there are no controlled data to prove it, my own experience, as well as that of several other trumpeters I know, is that flapping has some restorative effects. If I remember to do it right before I start playing, I find it easier to do my warm-up exercises. Also, in the middle of a gig, flapping during rest periods seems to help me get through the high note passages. I suspect flapping may increase blood flow through the lips, but this is just conjecture. One thing for certain is that, at worst, flapping is harmless. My advice is to give it a try and see if it helps.

Despite the volumes written about the embouchure, I think, in summary, we're left with a few simple principles: (1) Put the mouthpiece on the lips in a way that's comfortable, usually less on the upper than on the lower lip. (2) Find a mouthpiece that's both comfortable and effective, with regard to range, tone quality, intonation, and articulation. I suggest first determining what size (inside diameter) of rim is best for you and then trying several mouthpieces having similar rim sizes but differing in other ways: thick vs. thin rim; flat vs. rounded; V cup vs. bowl cup; shallow vs. deep cup; tight vs. open backbore etc. (3) Learn to breathe from your abdomen and to keep your throat open (if you can find it, I strongly recommend reading *The Tasteebros Way*). Although I haven't mentioned it before, any daily regimen of whole body physical exercise (for example, jogging, bicycling etc.) will obviously increase your lung capacity and be good for your breathing; and, conversely, smoking is an obvious negative. And (4), experiment with lip exercises (buzzing and especially flapping) that may help you maintain healthy and optimally functioning lips.

Warm-ups

The purpose of warm-up exercises is just that—to warm up to the point where you can play as well as you're capable of playing. After warming up, other exercises might be practiced with another goal in mind, for example improving your articulation, flexibility, and double or triple tonguing. However, warm-ups don't have to be meaningless, in the sense that, aside from warming up, something useful can also be accomplished at the same time. Opinions vary on how long one should spend on warming up. In my own experience, 12-15 minutes is optimal. Remember, I'm assuming that, on a daily basis, you only have 1-2 hours available for playing the trumpet.

My warm-up routine, which evolved over the course of two years, briefly touches a number of bases. I start with pedal tones, going down chromatically from middle C to double pedal C (that is, to an octave and a half lower than the ordinary range of the instrument). Then I reverse and ascend chromatically from double pedal C to middle C. I do this three or four times. Double pedal C and pedal C (both fingered with all three valves down) are the toughest notes to hit, and frankly I don't worry about whether I'm sharp or flat (usually) on them. The important thing to me about pedal tones is that they make my lip feel good. Next I do ascending arpeggios of dominant and minor seventh chords around the cycle of fifths. I'll talk more about the cycle of fifths in Part III. In the present context, I use the arpeggios as a way of getting the fingers and lips to work in sync while reinforcing the sounds of the most common chords. Sometimes I also play the chords in second and third inversions and/or in descending arpeggios. Following the same rationale, but for scales, I next play major scales, both ascending and descending, in five keys (C, G, F, Bb, and D) and in two octaves.

The following two exercises I do are based on *The Tasteebros Way*. The first of these is designed to reinforce the use of the abdominal muscles. Using solely my abdomen, without tonguing, I slur (slowly) from a G to a C (both in the staff) repeatedly, for 100-150 times. Then, to strengthen the corners of my mouth, I hold a G for as long as I can hold it, breathe through my nose (so my lips don't move), and hold the G again; and then repeat again. Although the Tasteebros recommend doing this for 20 minutes, I usually do it for no more than 3 minutes.

The last part of the warm-up routine entails a couple of flexibility exercises. The first starts with slurring from low F# to C# (four times), and then ascending chromatically, each time slurring to the next highest note with the same fingering; when I reach C, I descend down chromatically back to F#. The second flexibility exercise also starts with low F#, but this time slurring up to the next two highest notes with the same fingering (two times), and then ascending/descending chromatically up/down and to/from C as with the previous exercise. I also usually do what I call "footnotes" to the warm-up routine. First, simply for relaxation, I play the blues scales around the cycle of fifths, and finally, if I'm feeling good, I do a range check. That is, starting with G above the staff, I ascend to the highest note I can reach, which is usually G above high C. Now I'm ready to start playing/practicing for real.

My warm-up routine isn't for everyone; in fact it may only be best for me. However, making sure that some common elements are covered, I think everyone should be able to work out their own best routine. That is, all such routines should probably include some pedal tones (to get the lips vibrating in a relaxed way), some exercises to help the fingers and lips work in synchrony, some breathing exercises involving the abdomen, some work on strengthening the mouth corners, and some flexibility studies. Although there are many books that focus on one or more of these areas, remember that the whole routine shouldn't take too long (15 minutes maximum). After all you don't want your optimal playing condition to be wasted just on warm-up exercises.

Practicing

Ultimately, we all want to play music, and play it better than we do now. But in between warm-ups and playing music, we may want to learn or improve a particular technique or skill, for example, double or triple or legato tonguing, range expansion, use of the plunger mute etc. My advice is to pick one such goal for each practice session and focus on that. Appropriate exercises can be found in many books. In this section, by practicing, I mean practicing playing music. I'm assuming that you have at least a modicum of technical abilities and, if not, or if there are particular deficiencies here and there, that you've already spent some time (probably 15-20 minutes) working on the appropriate techniques immediately after warm-ups.

As the subtitle of this book indicates, I'm preoccupied with jazz. If Maurice Andre was your idol, and you're primarily interested in playing classical music, I suggest you look elsewhere for guidance. Also, jazz is a broad topic, and my reference to it is meant to be fairly but not totally inclusive, covering traditional (New Orleans, Dixieland, blues), swing, mainstream, bebop, and hard bop. I'm going to leave post bop and avante-garde as well as "classical" jazz (1920's) for someone else to deal with in a practical way. I suppose my personal bias is that "jazz has to swing," a la Wynton Marsalis. I'm not saying this to be critical, but rather to make it clear what I am and am not going to cover. In part III we will deal with jazz theory and its application, focusing mostly on improvisation. This section is more concerned with the mechanics of how to use your daily practice time to the most advantage.

Within the jazz limits I've set above, there are basically three kinds of musical tasks we need to practice. The first is playing arrangements. While small groups or combos may or may not use arrangements, big bands (10+ members) virtually always use arrangements; and arrangements can be difficult, far more difficult than the straight versions of the songs on which they're based. However, playing songs themselves, or rather the melodies of songs, isn't necessarily easy; playing a slow ballad with feeling and expression can be a challenge unto itself. The last of our three tasks, improvisation, is the most complicated one and the one that is hardest to define in terms of end points; that is, it may not be clear how to practice an improvised section nor how to know when progress is being made.

Let's deal with arrangements first. More than the notes themselves, timing can be the biggest obstacle to playing an arrangement correctly. And correct timing is the key to making an arrangement sound terrific. Even if there are some wrong notes, when everyone in a big band plays everything in time, and at the right time, the band sounds fantastic. A single missed beat can spoil the whole song. For example, in the most popular arrangement of Glen Miller's *In The Mood*, about three-quarters through the tune, just after the trumpet solo, there are three places where the drummer has to make a single loud bang on the fourth beat of a measure. If the drummer misses just one of these, or makes the strike early or late, the result is disaster. A similar situation can occur for trumpeters, where a single note may indicate a major transition—in the rhythm, melody or harmony. More commonly, timing problems appear with regard to a whole passage or section of a tune. When I started playing with a big band, in my first year as a comeback player, I encountered tremendous difficulty in playing the well known trumpet solo in *In The Mood*. I played all of the notes correctly but I just couldn't get the feel of it. Eventually, much to my chagrin, the band's director took the solo away from me. Two years later, when the person who had been playing the solo was ill, I was asked to give it a try. Much to everyone's delight, and my own amazement, it sounded great—and

I continued to play it with the band thereafter. So, what happened? Without even realizing it, I had learned how to "swing," and swing appropriately.

Practicing arrangements has two facets: the notes and the rhythm. As my own example illustrates, the former is usually easier to master than the latter. If you play something over and over again enough times, the notes will not be a problem—sooner or later. But if all you do is play something over and over again, the rhythm may be a problem forever. Listening, and then playing along while listening, is the key. Listening to a recording of how it's supposed to sound can be helpful; and if you play along with the recording a few times (or perhaps many times), you will indeed master the tune. This has worked for me on countless occasions with "big band" music—playing along with Ellington, Glen Miller, Woody Herman and even modern big bands (for example, the BBC Big Band is terrific) has made the learning process almost easy.

Compared to practicing an arrangement, practicing the original or "straight" version of a song is much easier—at least in theory. There are relatively few jazz tunes that pose a technical challenge—Clifford Brown's *Joy Spring* might be one. The real challenge is to play a tune with feeling and emotion, maintaining good intonation and using the most appropriate articulation (frequently legato). Listening is the key here as well—listen over and over again to whom you would most want to mimic. When you think you've got it, record yourself and compare it to the real thing. Listening to a recording of yourself can be a little unnerving. You will hear aspects of your playing of which you were never before aware—and you won't like many, or probably most, of these. But that's okay because now you know what needs work. In time the balance will shift and you will begin to look forward to listening to your own recording.

Now let's deal with improvisation, the most difficult thing to practice. Indeed, practicing improvisation almost seems like a contradiction in terms. Improvisation is supposed to be spontaneous. We'll talk about jazz theory and its application to improvisation in Part III—here the issue is focused solely on practicing. Playing along with CD's or online recordings is the solution here again. There are in fact three kinds of CD's that are useful in this regard: play-along CD's that are intended specifically for this purpose, CD's of combos that do not include your particular instrument, and CD's of musicians you want to emulate.

The Jamey Aebersold series of "Play-A-Long" CD's, now numbering over 130, is the indisputable leader in the field. Although there are many other play-along CD's on the market, most of them do not come close to providing a resource of a quality comparable to Aerbersold. The musical accompaniment on an Aerbersold CD is generally excellent, and the allowance for multiple choruses, sometimes with varying rhythms, is extremely helpful. However, even Aebersold is not perfect. Occasionally the rhythms seem too fast or too slow or too erratic (for example, in *Four*); and sometimes the songs are not transcribed in their correct (original) format (for example, the use of dotted eighth and sixteenth notes instead of straight, swing eighth notes in *Satin Doll*). About the most disturbing thing I've ever found is that, in three Miles Davis tunes (*Solar*, *Blue in Green*, and *Freddie Freeloader*), the original endings are missing altogether. But aside from these infrequent oversights, the Aerbersold recordings can't be beat. They allow you to practice your improvisations with a real combo—it's the next best thing to playing with a live combo.

Tragically, not every professional jazz combo or ensemble includes a trumpeter. However, for comeback trumpet players, this glaring omission can be quite useful. Playing along with a CD of a trio that includes piano, bass and drums can, depending on the CD, be even more instructive than an Aebersold CD. While the Aebersold recordings make room for another instrument, you have to be more inventive as well as more melodic to fit in with a real CD. If you do this enough, you will likely discover who you enjoy playing with most; and this should help you in developing your own voice and style. My favorite person to play with is Oscar Peterson.

Playing along with your favorite trumpet players is perhaps the most challenging of these exercises. The idea is to both mimic and complement what's being played on the CD. Some CD's and trumpeters are easier to play along with than others. It helps to use CD's that leave some "space" for another instrument. I've played along with Chet Baker, Miles Davis, Kenny Dorham, Clark Terry, Art Farmer and Clifford Brown among others. When you play along with the "greats" you will hear aspects of their styles that you hadn't noticed previously. This is especially true for articulation and phrasing. Eventually you will be able to sound somewhat like them, and your own voice will begin to emerge as you combine different elements from different players.

Lastly, before closing this section, mention should be made of a couple of other very useful play-along resources. PG Music's *Band-in-a-Box* (updated almost every year) is a wonderful computer program that allows you to compose and modify songs, download midi files of songs, and have the computer play songs; and you can have the computer play with a wide variety of instruments, rhythms, tempos, and key signatures. There are thousands of free downloadable songs for *Band-in-a-Box* on the internet. The quality of the programmed instrumentation varies but most of them are done very well. This means that you can almost always find an accompaniment with which to practice an improvisation—and you can also build the world's largest fake book. I use this program every day. Another useful computer program is Roni Music's *Amazing Slow Downer*. This program allows you to slow down any audio CD or MP3 file—and it does so without distortion and without changing the pitch. There are several other programs on the market that claim to do this, but in my opinion this is the best. In view of these programs and many other music resources on the internet, including Google Play, Spotify, and numerous YouTube videos, I think there's little doubt that the computer has increasingly become the comeback trumpet player's best friend.

PART III: JAZZ THEORY AND JAZZ

About twenty years ago, when I started reading jazz theory, I was amazed at the complexity of the subject. Although I knew something about chords, having dabbled on the piano from time to time, I didn't know that chords had anything to do with playing the trumpet. As I mentioned earlier, my formal and former trumpet training, while growing up, was all technical and oriented toward playing classical music. I liked jazz but apparently never had a trumpet teacher that did. For nearly 50 years I erroneously believed that improvisation was totally based on playing by ear; and because I couldn't do it very well when I was young (although I only tried a few times), I believed that my ears were simply not up to the task. A couple of years and many books later, a whole new world of music opened up for me. I'm still no Clifford Brown, but I play better than I ever imagined possible when I was younger. Ear training was certainly part of the reason for this, but it was a growing knowledge of jazz theory that gave me the tools to make the best use of my ears.

It's indeed possible to improvise well based on ears alone—but this is a rare exception. The best example is Chet Baker—you probably already know more about chords and chord progressions than he did. At the other extreme, Miles Davis was a musical intellectual—he knew everything about chords and chord progressions. The interesting thing is that Chet Baker and Miles Davis sometimes sounded similar; in fact one was occasionally accused of imitating the other. What's interesting is that the same or similar result was achieved by very different approaches. The best solution, at least for the vast majority of us, is to combine both approaches—this means nurturing your ears and expanding your mind.

In discussing jazz theory, I'm going to refer to a few other books. None of them tell you how to improvise. They provide sets of rules to follow and principles to use; they may also give you examples of improvised tunes and suggest ways of creating patterns and licks. The challenge is to find a way of using this information in a way that is uniquely your own. What I've found is that some rules, principles, and suggestions are more practical than others. I'm going to attempt to tell you what I've learned and how I learned it.

In my opinion, *The Jazz Theory Book* by Mark Levine is the best book of its kind, being both complete and clearly written; there are many competitors, some which I will mention in due course. A nice companion to Levine's book, particularly for trumpet players, is *Jazz Tactics* by Chase Sanborn. I've read *The Jazz Theory Book* six times, and each time I absorb a little more from it. In about 500 pages (but with large print) Levine presents all (or certainly almost all) of the elements to be considered in constructing an improvised solo. He never tells you how to create the solo, just how to find the pool of notes from which to choose in a particular circumstance (for example, when covering a major versus a minor II-V-I progression; II-V-I will be defined below). On the other hand, *Jazz Tactics*, perhaps because it's written by a trumpet player, actually provides some useful hints as to how to go about choosing notes for a solo. However, like every other jazz author, both Levine and Sanborn transcend the practical limitations of ordinary mortals (amateurs like us) and give us enough instructions to keep us practicing at least 12 hours a day (the technical term for this is "woodshedding"). So, what can we distill from their and others' advice that's reasonable?

First let's consider what's unreasonable. Virtually every book I've read about jazz improvisation stresses the importance of learning everything "in all 12 keys." Typically, a recommended exercise is written out in the key of C and the reader is instructed to master the exercise in every key. Is this really necessary? Well maybe for a professional, but definitely not for an advanced amateur. To make this point, I checked the key signature of 100 tunes selected at random from the much larger book of tunes that my jazz combo used; and I transposed the key up a step for Bb instruments. It turned out that seven keys accounted for 98 of the 100 tunes; and they're probably the ones that you've already predicted: C, F, Bb, Eb, D, G, and A. *Take Five* and *Round Midnight* in Ab (Fm) were the exceptions. Okay, so now you're thinking I picked out easy tunes; or you've recalled that the key signature isn't always the key center for all parts of a tune. Both objections may be well founded, but my point is that there's a lot of music you can play with seven keys. And if you encounter a tune with four or five sharps or flats, you just need to work a little harder once in a while; and indeed, improvising credibly on *Take Five* has been one of the more difficult tasks I've tackled.

Authors' instructions to practice, practice and practice are not just restricted to mastering the 12 keys. Even if confined to a single key, the directions in any one book on improvisation would probably take a lifetime of free time if you were to follow them exactly as prescribed. For example, Hal Crook's *How to Improvise* focuses on learning one thing at a time and recommends practice sessions lasting only two hours. Although, compared to others, the requirements of this approach are modest, there are so many different things to practice in Crook's book that it's not even close to being practical. Perhaps there might be enough time for this if you were starting at age 10, but certainly not if you're a comeback player starting at age 40 or 50 or 60.

In pursuing the issue of what's reasonable, I'm going to first outline what I think are the basic steps towards being able to improvise in a pleasing, if not perfect, way. Then, with reference to other books, I will discuss some of the more advanced topics that are, at this point in time, beyond my own abilities. You can then decide for yourself whether the latter are worthy of your effort or not.

Learning scales and chords

Nothing is more basic than scales and chords, the notes of which make up all melodies and harmonies. Becoming intimately familiar with chords is essential for creating any decent improvisation that is not based on ear alone. Chord tones are the most harmonic notes, often the "essential" or "target" notes that make an improvised phrase sound complete. And knowledge of the scales from which the chords are derived is essential for defining the pools of notes that span "cadences" or chord progressions.

Major scales, and the chords based on them, are by far the most useful. Each major scale has seven modes, each having a strange Greek name—Ionian, Dorian, Phrygian, Lydian, Mixolydian, Aeolian, and Locrian. The first time I heard these names, I thought it was some kind of a joke. However, the more I read the more I found out that people actually use them, which means you need to learn them! The 1st, 3rd, 5th and 7th note of each mode produces a series of commonly used 7th chords—major, minor, dominant and half-diminished. Beyond this, more complicated nuances occur when "extensions" (9th, 11th, and 13th) are included. The complete series of chords in the key of C, in order of their modes of origin, then becomes Ionian C major 7th (Cmaj7), Dorian D minor 7th (Dm7), Phrygian E sus $b9^{th}$ (Esus^{b9}), Lydian F major augmented 4th or 11th (Fmaj$^{\#4}$), Mixolydian G dominant 7th (G7), Aeolian A minor $b6^{th}$ or $b13^{th}$ (Am^{b6}), and B Locrian half-diminished (BØ) or minor $7^{th}b5^{th}$ (Bm7^{b5}). Also, note that with reference to the order of their modes, chord qualities are frequently designated by roman numerals. A I chord is a major 7th, a II chord is a minor 7th, a V chord is a dominant 7th etc. The most common chord progression, used in countless tunes, is the major II-V-I. Fortunately, all of the notes in a II-V-I progression come from the same major scale, although from three different modes (same notes but starting at a different place). This means that if you know the major scale from which the I chord is derived, you already know the pool of "inside" notes available for use while improvising over the three chords (we'll get to "outside" notes later). However, all notes of even the correct scales or modes are not created equal. The fourth note (F in the key of C) of the first mode, the fourth note (C in the key of C) of the fifth mode, and the second note (C in the key of C) of the seventh mode are commonly referred to as "avoid" notes because they sound dissonant when played over their respective chords (Cmaj7, G7, and BØ, respectively). At the other extreme, chord tones usually require special emphasis because they are the most consonant sounding notes and therefore the most "essential" and defining sounds of an improvised sequence. However, even the roles of chord tones may differ. Thirds and sevenths define the qualities of chords: a major or minor 3rd distinguishes major from minor chords, and a major or minor 7th distinguishes major from dominant chords.

Thirds and sevenths often require "resolution" or return to a "target" note, commonly the 1st or the 5th of a major or dominant chord.

It's not my purpose here to review all scales and chords (which can be found in many other texts), but rather to indicate what I think is most important and useful. Compared to a major scale, a minor-major scale (also called a melodic minor scale) has a flatted 3rd; and each minor-major scale, like its major counterpart, has seven modes. The sixth and seventh melodic minor modes are particularly interesting, containing the notes for half-diminished and altered dominant chords, respectively. Note, therefore, that you can play the seventh mode of a major scale (see above) or the sixth mode of a melodic minor scale to cover a half-diminished chord—and the latter is usually preferable to the former, because half-diminished chords are more commonly part of minor chord progressions. The altered dominant chord (for example, C7alt) can have an augmented 5th and an augmented 9th as well as a diminished 5th and a diminished 9th; it's used in minor chord progressions as well as a substitute for a dominant chord in major chord progressions.

There are two sets of diminished scales—half-whole and whole-half, meaning that the scales comprise notes ascending in alternating half and whole steps, with one set starting in half steps and the other set starting in whole steps; and there are only three distinct scales in each set. Both whole-half and half-whole diminished scales can be played over diminished 7th chords, the notes of which ascend in minor 3rd steps. The half-whole diminished scale can also be played over a dominant 7th chord with a flatted 9th (for example, $C7^{b9}$).

Possibly the most important and most useful scales to learn are the blues scales, six note scales containing a root, a flatted 3rd, a 4th, a raised 4th, a 5th, and a flatted 7th (for example, C, Eb, F, F#, G, Bb). Blues scales are of course most commonly played over blues' progressions, of which there are many (both major and minor). Although in this instance it's not difficult to learn the blues scales in all 12 keys, concert Bb (C for trumpet) and F (G for trumpet) are the most frequently used keys for blues' tunes. Closely related to the blues scales, and more or less interchangeable with them, are minor pentatonic scales, five note scales that are the same as the blues scales but without the raised 4th (for example, C, Eb, F, G, Bb). We'll talk more about other pentatonic scales (major and altered) later, when discussing ways of covering chord progressions.

There are a variety of other scales (for example, whole tone, bebop, harmonic major and minor etc.), and I will mention some of them later in specific contexts (for example, the use of the harmonic minor scale to cover a minor II-V-I progression). For present purposes, however, if you know the scales I've listed above in seven keys (and maybe just two keys for the blues), you're in good shape—and you will have a wealth of music from which to choose.

The cycle of fifths (or fourths)

Perhaps nothing in jazz is more basic than the cycle of fifths, also called the cycle of fourths. If you start with C and go up in fourths, you end up with the following: C, F, Bb, Eb, Ab, C#, F#, B, E, A, D, G, and back to C. If you start with C and go down in fifths, the cycle is the same. If you start at the other end and go backwards, the cycle ascends in fifths and descends in fourths (C, G, D, A etc.). The forward version of the cycle contains a number of commonly used chord progressions; for example, any three consecutive roots in the cycle can be used to form a II-V-I. (minor, dominant, major) progression and any four consecutive roots can be used to form a III-VI-II-V progression, often used as a "turnaround" prior to repeating the first section of a tune. If there is one thing that you should truly internalize to the point of becoming automatic, it is the cycle of fifths. I recommend doing all practicing of scales and chords in the order of the cycle of fifths (forward version).

Contour, rhythm and essential tones

Jerry Coker wrote a classic book, titled *Improvising* Jazz, in 1964. It's only 115 pages (inclusive of 35 pages of appendix), and the pages are small (6⅛ x 9¼ inches). Chapter 9, only nine pages in length, is the most important part of the book—and possibly the most important nine pages of any book on jazz improvisation. Focusing on motif development, Coker describes how contour, rhythm and essential tones each contribute to the unique character of a melodic line; and he illustrates how an improvised line can be constructed by varying one of these elements at a time. Contour refers to the relative directions of pitches, for example, a phrase that starts with a sustained (two beats or more) high note descending stepwise with eighth notes and ending with a sustained low note. Rhythm is perhaps self-evident, incorporating a repetitive pattern of notes and rests. Essential tones are the critical notes of a phrase, the ones that are emphasized and make a phrase memorable.

Of the three Coker elements, I find it most useful to keep the rhythm constant and vary the contour and/or essential pitches. This works very well for tunes having very distinctive contours and/or very obvious essential pitches. For example, the instantly recognizable contour of *Doxy* (Miles Davis) makes it easy to improvise a solo that maintains the contour and rhythm while changing the essential pitches. On the other hand, a few essential pitches in *All of Me* (Marks/Simons) define the tune's progression, and this makes it easy to improvise a contour-based solo while retaining those essential pitches as well as the rhythm. This approach doesn't work all of the time, but it works enough of the time to be remarkably effective. It makes it possible for even a novice, lacking extensive knowledge of scales, chords and progressions, to solo credibly on at least a few tunes.

By the way, it should be noted that Jerry Coker has written several books over the last 40 years, including a "comprehensive approach" to improvisation. In general I can't say that I've found any of these to be particularly useful, or at least none as useful as Chapter 9 in *Improvising Jazz*.

Jazz rhythm

Before proceeding further, a rhythmic digression is in order. The rhythm most typical of jazz is a combination of swing and syncopation. In a swing rhythm, each pair of eighth notes should be treated like a triplet, with the first eighth note having the duration of the first two notes of a triplet and the second eighth note having the duration of the third note of a triplet. Sometimes a swing rhythm is erroneously indicated in the written music by converting the first eighth note to a dotted eighth note and the second eighth note to a sixteenth note. The best way to write music with a swing rhythm is to write the notes "straight" (equal eighth notes) and indicate at the start of the tune that it is to be played with swing or with a "swing feel."

Syncopation usually means that upbeats are emphasized or accented; and rests frequently appear after as well as before such notes. Furthermore, although downbeats 1 and 3 are harmonically the strong beats, accenting downbeats 2 and 4 adds to the feel of syncopation. Hence a typical or prototypical jazz rhythm combines swing eighth notes along with an emphasis on upbeats and on downbeats 2 and 4. However, in terms of the melodic content of an improvised motif, downbeats 1 and 3 are most important and sound best when played with chord tones.

Chromaticism

The chromatic scale, containing all 12 notes, can be a useful and relatively simple device for improvising interesting lines on any chord or chord progression. In essence, multiple "passing notes" are used to connect distant chord tones. The important caution here is to use chromaticism sparingly and appropriately (or maybe "tastefully" would be a better word). Clifford Brown excelled at doing this and indeed his tune *Joy Spring* can almost be considered a chromatic invitation. When applied in moderation, chromatic runs or sequences can transform a relatively dull solo into one that is inventive if not exciting; but used in excess, chromaticism can be lethal. Like anything else, some practice is required to find out what sounds appropriate (or tasteful).

"Special effects"

A number of fairly easy manipulations, or "special effects," can add interest and innovation to a solo. These include long tones, trills, repeated notes, glissandos (glisses), slow valve releases, and a variety of sounds created with the use of the plunger mute. Just holding a note for a long period of time (8 beats or more) can sometimes sound remarkably beautiful. The trick is to pick the right effect to use at the right time and place; and the right effect may be different for different players. For example, Freddie Hubbard was a master at using repeated note sequences. It's probably best to become adept at using two or three of these special effects and learn to use them wisely and sparingly. The result should become integrated as part of "your" sound, helping you to become distinctive if not unique.

Playing the changes: vertical vs. horizontal

Most books on jazz improvisation stress horizontal playing over chord changes. This means finding the scale or scales that cover a chord progression and using the notes of those scales as the "pool" of notes from which to create improvised lines. In the case of modal tones, where one chord (usually a Dorian minor) spans several measures, horizontal playing (usually using the Dorian scale) is a virtual requirement. However, when chord durations are only two or four beats, it's possible to play vertically, focusing almost exclusively on chord tones instead of the scales from which the chords are derived. Indeed, playing just the 3rds and 7ths of chords, referred to as guide tones, can sometimes produce an alternate melody that is both interesting and harmonious. Aside from creating more inventive and imaginative solos, one often-stated advantage of playing horizontally is that it's easier: you supposedly don't need to think and respond as quickly because the same scale can cover several chords, whereas playing vertically requires immediate access to rapidly changing chord tones. At least this is the "party line" espoused in a number of books on improvisation. Personally, I have not always found this to be the case, as often I can think of the chord tones faster than I can determine the appropriate scale to cover several chords. The real advantage of horizontal vs. vertical playing is that the scales provide more notes, thereby enabling more creative solos with more variety. In this context it should also be noted that the melodies and harmonies of many tunes (for example, *Memories of You*) stay entirely within the key signature; that is, there are no accidentals (sharps or flats) and no modulations to other keys. This usually means that one set of scales (modes) can be applied to the whole tune—so at least the primary pool of useable notes is easily known. It's therefore a good idea to make a quick check for accidentals before starting to work on a new tune.

Inside vs. outside

With regard to improvisation, inside and outside refer, respectively, to playing licks and motifs consistent with the present chords and scales (or playing diatonic to the current key center) or inconsistent with the present chords and scales (or playing nondiatonic to the current key center). The "present chords and scales" usually consist of a progression of two or more chords, with a major II-V-I progression being the most common and the key center being determined by the I chord. Inside-outside-inside is the general rule for incorporating outside playing. That is, outside licks create interest by virtue of their contrast from the preceding inside lines; and outside licks eventually become satisfying to the ear when they resolve to subsequent inside lines. It's not easy to do this, at least in a way that sounds thoughtful and appropriate. If it's done carelessly, the result can be disastrous (and I speak from experience). My advice is to only attempt outside playing on tunes that you know exceptionally well. The overriding concern here (or at least my overriding concern) is to produce musical music—and I am admittedly biased against some of the "free" jazz of the avant-garde.

Pentatonic shortcuts

Pentatonic scales are five note scales that can be played over a number of common chord progressions. They can be thought of as shortcuts in the sense that it may be easier to focus on playing five notes across two or three chords than playing seven or more notes depending on whether the progression is approached vertically or horizontally. Note that I say "may be easier." That is, the experts (professionals) state unequivocally that it **is** easier although personally I have not often found this to be the case. I usually think of chord tones and their seven note scales before I think of the most applicable pentatonic scales. And because the applicable pentatonic scales are always contained within the appropriate chord scales, the advantage of pentatonic thinking has largely eluded me. Nevertheless, some experts place an enormous emphasis on pentatonics. In particular, George Bouchard (*Intermediate Jazz Improvisation*) has devised a remarkably inclusive approach to using pentatonics in a plethora of improvising situations.

There are both major and minor pentatonic scales. The major pentatonic scales consist of the root, and a major 2nd, 3rd, 5th and 6th (for example, C, D, E, G, A). The minor pentatonic scales consist of the root, a flatted 3rd, a 4th, a 5th, and a flatted 7th (for example, C, Eb, F, G, Bb). In addition, Bouchard makes use of what he refers to as "altered" pentatonic scales, consisting of the root, a major 2nd, a flatted 3rd, a 5th and a 6th.

The minor II-V-I

Perhaps one of the most controversial topics in jazz theory books is how to cover a minor II-V-I progression. While a single major scale will cover a major II-V-I, this is not the case for a minor II-V-I. This is because each of the chords of a minor II-V-I has a different and unique origin. In a minor II-V-I, the II chord is a half-diminished chord, derived either from the VIIth (Locrian) major mode or the VIth melodic minor mode; the V chord is an altered dominant chord, derived from the VIIth melodic minor mode, or a dominant b9 chord, derived from the half-whole diminished scale; and the I is a minor-major chord, derived from the I melodic minor mode (or sometimes it's possible to substitute a minor 7th chord or a minor 6th chord). While there is no single scale that completely covers all three chords of the minor II-V-I, the harmonic minor scale of the tonic (I) comes close. The harmonic minor scale is a seven-note scale with a flatted 3rd and a flatted 6th; that is, there is a root, a 2nd, a flatted 3rd, a 4th, a 5th, a flatted 6th, and a 7th. The C harmonic minor scale therefore includes an Eb and an Ab. While Eb and Ab are not both contained in all three of the chords (or scales of origin) of a C minor II-V-I (DØ, G7alt, Cm^{maj7}), one or the other of these notes is contained in each of the three chords. Although the fit is close, close is not good enough for many, and there is considerable controversy as to whether or not the harmonic minor scale should be used in this fashion. In fact, in his 1999 book, *Clear Solutions for Jazz Improvisers*, Jerry Coker devotes a whole chapter to explaining why the harmonic minor scale should not be used this way. Mark Levine (*The Jazz Theory Book*) provides a shorter explanation for this while, on the contrary, George Bouchard ((*Intermediate Jazz Improvisation*) mentions, almost in passing, that the harmonic minor scale **is** to played over a minor II-V-I. Bouchard also offers a pentatonic solution to this problem, suggesting that the minor II-V (for example, DØ , G7alt) can also be covered with two altered pentatonics, the first having a root beginning on the third of the II chord (F of DØ) and the second having a root a half step up from the root of the V chord (Ab of G7alt); a minor major scale or a minor scale would then be used for resolution to the I chord (Cm^{maj7} or Cm).

Tension and release

A core principle of improvisation, as well as melody development in general, is that interest is generated to the extent that the melodic line incorporates tension and release. That is, analogous to a novel (or a short story), motifs are more likely to sound interesting/creative/appealing when they use tension to build a sense of mystery and release or resolution to provide a solution or ending to the mystery. Tension is created with the use of non-chord and non-diatonic notes, together referred to as non-harmonic tones; release occurs when the non-harmonic tones resolve, usually in whole or half steps, to a chord tone, sometimes referred to as a target note. While different jazz authors stress this topic to varying extents, Jimmy Amadie's book (*Jazz Improv: How to Play It and Teach It!*) focuses almost exclusively on tension and release—it is the cornerstone of his entire system of improvisation. Although this may be overdoing it a bit, there is no disputing the importance of the basic concept.

THE END *(really the end of the beginning, or maybe the end of the middle)*

Tension and release is probably an appropriate place to end this treatise. The tensions associated with transforming a comeback trumpet player into a good trumpet player are never ending, as for example, when a pivotal high note in a solo is missed; but fortunately, the releases occur more and more frequently as well, for example, when an improvised solo really sounds credible. I am constantly discovering new nuances in my playing technique, new ways of approaching improvisation, and even new equipment (a piccolo trumpet and a bass trumpet). This may be the end of my memoirs for now, but certainly not the end.

Stanley D. Glick
Lutz, FL
January, 2017

About the Author

Stanley D. Glick, Ph.D., M.D. (Albert Einstein College of Medicine, 1969, 1971)

From 2000 until my retirement in June of 2014, I was the Director of the Center for Neuropharmacology and Neuroscience at Albany Medical College. Before then I was Chair of the Department of Pharmacology and Neuroscience (1995-2000) and Chair of the Department of Pharmacolgoy and Toxicology (1984-95). Prior to joining Albany Medical College, I was a professor of pharmacology at Mount Sinai School of Medicine (1971-1984).

My major research interest focuses on the neurobiology of drug addiction. I am co-inventor of 18-methoxycoronaridine (18-MC), a novel agent for treating drug addiction. 18-MC is likely to be useful in treating multiple forms of drug abuse, including opioid and stimulant dependence, alcoholism and smoking. Other studies indicate that it may also be useful in treating obesity.

I have authored or co-authored over 480 experimental papers, reviews and abstracts. My first novel, *N Equals One*, was published in October of 2014.

I began playing trumpet at age 6 and, by the time I was 8 or 9, I was the only soloist at the annual spring school concert. I played with various orchestras in my teens and spent one summer playing Sunday concerts at resort sites around the perimeter of Lake Placid. When I was 15, I was in a trumpet trio that played in several regional talent contests. As a result of winning a couple of these, we were invited to appear on the Ted Mac Amateur Hour, a popular TV show in the 1950's. After that I played with a Dixieland jazz group and with my college's orchestra in my freshman year. The trumpet was relegated to the closet by my sophomore year. Being a serious pre-med student took over my life; and the pursuit of science and raising a family followed. For the next 35 years, I usually took the trumpet out of its case once every 6-9 months, played it for about 20 minutes, and then returned it to the closet.

In the late fall of 1997 I received an email from a colleague soliciting people to join a big band, eventually named the Swing Docs. My youngest child had just gone away to college, and I was looking for something new to do outside of the lab and office. I was already in the midst of rejuvenating my interest in music and, for more than a year, had been spending a couple of hours every week or two listening to new jazz releases at Borders and purchasing a CD or two. Thus, I was well primed when this email arrived. I told my colleague that I had barely played for 35 years but that I would give it a try if he was willing to put up with me; I'm quite grateful that he agreed to give me a chance. The initial experience of playing with a group after so many years was exhilarating. I bought a new trumpet after a few weeks and started practicing at least an hour a day; sometimes this occurred even late at night after returning home from a long meeting at work. While it wasn't too difficult to get my lip back in shape, learning to read music again and keep in time was more of a challenge. The first year I spent most of my practice sessions simply trying to cope with the printed notes. Thereafter I focused more on improving my technique and on learning the chord/scale rudiments of improvisation.

In 1999 I started a jazz/swing combo (quintet plus vocalist), eventually named FIVE+1. Between the two bands I usually had about 30 gigs each year. I played with both the Swing Docs and FIVE+1 until the middle of 2015, when I moved to the Tampa Bay area of Florida. I'm now playing with a trio (guitar, bass and flugelhorn) and with a new big band. I think I'm hooked on music for life.

Printed in Great Britain
by Amazon